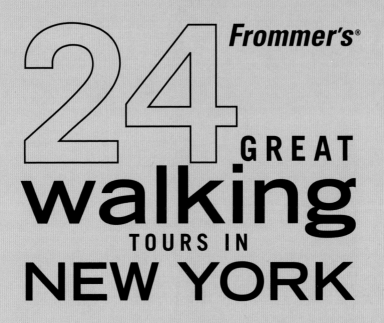

Frommer's®

24 GREAT walking TOURS IN NEW YORK

D1403459

WILEY

Wiley Publishing, Inc.

Authors: James and Michelle Nevius
Managing Editor: Paul Mitchell
Series Editor: Donna Wood
Art Editor: Alison Fenton
Copy Editor: Julia Canning
Proofreader: Sandy Draper
Picture Researcher: Joanne Forrest-Smith
Cartography provided by the Mapping Services
Department of AA Publishing
Image retouching and internal repro: Sarah Montgomery
Production: Stephanie Allen

Edited, designed and produced by AA Publishing.
© AA Media Limited 2008. Reprinted June 2009

Published by AA Publishing.

Published in the United States by
Wiley Publishing, Inc.
111 River Street, Hoboken, NJ 07030

Find us online at Frommers.com

Frommer's is a registered trademark of Arthur Frommer.
Used under license.
Mapping in this title produced from New York data
© Tele Atlas N.V. 2008 Tele Atlas

ISBN 978-0-470-22896-8

A04184

A CIP catalogue record for this book is available from the
British Library.

The contents of this publication are believed correct
at the time of printing. Nevertheless, the publishers
cannot accept responsibility for errors or omissions,
or for changes in details given in this guide or for
the consequences of any reliance on the information
provided by the same. Assessments of attractions and
so forth are based upon the author's own experience
and, therefore, descriptions given in this guide necessarily
contain an element of subjective opinion which may not
reflect the publishers' opinion or dictate a reader's own
experiences on another occasion.

Colour reproduction by Keene Group, Andover
Printed in China by Leo Paper Group

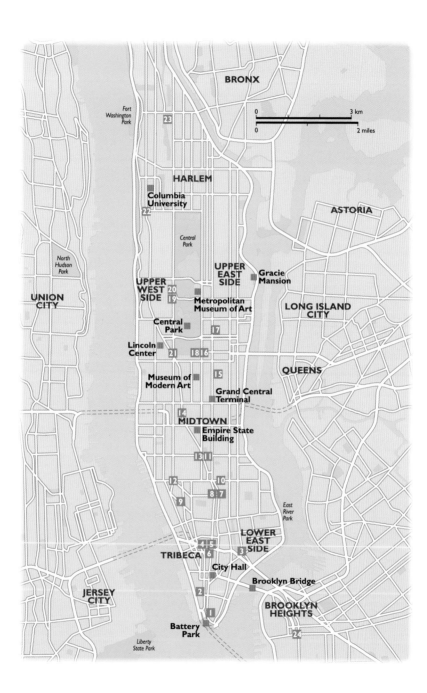

BRONX

Fort
Washington
Park

23

HARLEM

Columbia
University

22

Central
Park

North
Hudson
Park

UPPER
EAST
SIDE

Gracie
Mansion

UNION
CITY

UPPER
WEST
SIDE

20
19

Metropolitan
Museum of Art

LONG ISLAND
CITY

Central
Park

17

Lincoln
Center

21

18 16

QUEENS

Museum of
Modern Art

15

Grand Central
Terminal

14

MIDTOWN

Empire State
Building

13 11

12

10

8 7

9

East
River
Park

LOWER
EAST
SIDE

4 5

3

TRIBECA

6

City Hall

JERSEY
CITY

Brooklyn Bridge

BROOKLYN
HEIGHTS

2

1

Battery
Park

24

Liberty
State Park

ASTORIA

0   3 km

0   2 miles

CONTENTS

Introduction   6

1   Historic Lower Manhattan   8
2   In the Shadow of the Towers   14
3   The Jewish Lower East Side   22
4   East Meets West   28
5   Little Italy and NoLita   36
6   SoHo and TriBeCa   42
7   NoHo and the Notorious Bowery   50
8   Gilded Age Greenwich Village   56
9   Off the Grid in the West Village   64
10   From Prussians to Punks   70
11   Secrets of Gramercy Park   78
12   Chelsea Transformations   84
13   From Flatiron to Empire State   92
14   Across 42nd Street   98
15   Modern Midtown   106
16   The Silk Stocking District   112
17   The Architecture of Museum Mile   120
18   Landscape Versus Playground   126
19   From the Castle to the Woods   134
20   New York's Last Frontier   140
21   Artists' Upper West Side   148
22   Morningside Heights   154
23   Harlem and Hamilton Heights   160
24   America's First Suburb   166

Index   174
Acknowledgements   176

Introduction

Of all the cities in America, New York is the one best seen on foot. Indeed, the city was designed for walking—the Manhattan grid plan, with its abundance of river-to-river streets, was created so that everything important would be within walking distance of everything else. The result is a profusion of street life, where walking around any corner brings new and different delights.

The city's history long predates anything still visible, save for the geography of the island itself. For thousands of years, this island was known as *Manna Hatta*, a Native American term whose exact definition is unknown, but which probably describes its rocky, inhospitable nature (best seen today in Central Park).

The first European settlers were employees of the Dutch West India Company, who established a fur-trading venture here in 1621 and a colony called New Netherland. Its capital, New Amsterdam, was the area of Manhattan located below Wall Street. In 1664, the Dutch surrendered to troops sent by James, Duke of York, and the name changed to reflect the new royal patron. At the end of the American Revolution, New York was briefly the first US capital. When the politicians left in 1790, the city retained its role as the country's financial centre, a title it never lost.

The 19th century saw the city rise to prominence as America's major port, its largest city and the primary destination for immigrants—first Irish and German and then, in the Ellis Island years, Eastern European Jews and southern Italians. In the 20th century, the city expanded its borders to encompass the outer boroughs: Queens, Brooklyn, Staten Island and the Bronx. New immigrants arrived from every country of the globe. The 21st century began with the destruction of the World Trade Center, an event that will continue to shape the city's future for years to come.

New York is a city of neighbourhoods (Alistair Cooke called it the 'biggest collection of villages in the world') and the tours in this book are organized around well-known areas like Greenwich Village, SoHo, and Harlem. But the tours will take you into less touristy places as well, from the civic centre near the World Trade Center to the tree-lined streets of Brooklyn Heights. The city's history is often best revealed through its architecture, which comes in an abundance of styles, from Georgian vernacular to post-Post Modernism. There are far too many great buildings for us to possibly cover them all and, as you walk, you'll pass gorgeous architecture not mentioned in the text. It's our hope that you'll enjoy these varied streetscapes and that every road we take you down will offer something interesting, whether it is on the tour's itinerary or not.

There is a fair share of mystery, too. Some places are said to be haunted, and we point out the ones you'll be seeing. But the city also has its share of hidden history, and on each tour we've highlighted places with unusual stories to tell, or other well-kept secrets that might not be so easily discernable to the casual passerby.

Larger neighbourhoods have been divided into two walks. When possible, we've provided instructions on how to link these into one, longer tour. However, many walks start and end in close proximity to each other and you shouldn't have any trouble connecting many of these tours on your own, should you feel energetic enough to tackle more than one in a day.

Each walk begins at a subway station, and directions are provided to the station closest to the end of each route. Ongoing subway construction in Manhattan—usually taking place on weekends—can disrupt service; visit www.mta.info for up-to-date information before you set out.

Most of all—enjoy!

Historic Lower Manhattan

Explore the fascinating history of early New York, walking the same streets as Dutch traders and American revolutionaries.

To stroll around Lower Manhattan is to chart its earliest history—this was once the entire city. The streets tell overlapping stories of Manhattan's many peoples: long before Henry Hudson's arrival in 1609, the broad Wickquasgeck Trail led Native Americans into the island's lush interior. In the 1620s, Dutch settlers created New Amsterdam and the trail became the Heere Straat ('Gentleman's Street'). The street's width led to its nickname as the 'Breede Wegh' and when the English took the city for the Duke of York in 1664, this was translated into English – Broadway. New York thrived as a British colony, then the American Revolution split the city into Loyalists and Patriots. When the Patriots' cause prevailed, streets were renamed again—for example, Crown Street, just north of Wall Street, became Liberty. In 1785, the city became America's first federal capital and the fledgling nation's economic centre. To see this area in all its vibrancy, visit weekdays when the financial markets are trading. If you plan to visit the Statue of Liberty/Ellis Island, see them as early in the day as possible.

| Exit the 4/5 subway at Bowling
| Green. Directly in front of you is the
former US Custom House (now the
Museum of the American Indian).

This building, designed by Cass Gilbert,
opened in 1907 as the US Custom
House. At that time, nearly three quarters
of America's revenue was generated by
imports to New York, and the building's
iconography glorifies America as a world
trading power. Above the cornice stand
12 heroic figures representing the history
of trade, beginning with Athena and
ending with Queen Victoria on the right.
Flanking the entry staircase are figures by
Daniel Chester French of North America
(left; ready to move into the future) and
Europe (right; regal but fading into the
past). On the far ends sit Asia (meditating,
with a Buddha on her lap) and Africa
(simply asleep). Above each window
on the main rotunda floor is a face:
these symbolize the races of mankind,
a reminder that the goods shipped into
New York came from all corners of the
globe. Inside the building are Reginald
Marsh's murals of New York's bustling
port, and the exhibits of the the National
Museum of the American Indian.

**NATIONAL MUSEUM OF THE
AMERICAN INDIAN;**

DAILY 10-5; TEL: 212-514-3700; www.nmai.si.edu

2 Enter Bowling Green Park, which is
ringed by a wrought-iron fence.

Situated at the foot of Broadway, this was
the town square of New Amsterdam.
In 1733, it became the city's first park

WHERE TO EAT

🍴 FRAUNCES TAVERN,
54 Pearl Street (at Broad Street);
Tel: 212-968-1776.
Classic American cuisine.

🍴 CAFE DOPPIO,
55 Broad Street (entrance on
Beaver Street);
Tel: 212-785-7595.
Homemade soups, sandwiches
and Italian coffee.

🍴 FINANCIER,
62 Stone Street (at Mill Lane);
Tel: 212-344-5600.
Pastries and coffee with charming
tables outside.

and was used for lawn bowling. The
fence, dating back to 1771, was built
to protect a gilded equestrian statue
of George III which had been erected
here a year earlier. On 9 July 1776 the
Declaration of Independence was read
out and an angry mob stormed the
fence, toppled the king and melted the
statue into 40,088 bullets. The fence was
damaged, too: look closely and you'll see
that its finials were violently removed by
the revolutionaries. At the park's north
end sits Arturo DiModica's *Charging Bull*.
In 1989, DiModica secretly installed this
giant symbol of the rising stock market in
front of the New York Stock Exchange.
The unauthorized gift was moved to the
park 'temporarily' a few days later and has
been here ever since.

OPPOSITE: FEDERAL HALL

I

DISTANCE 1.15 miles (1.85km)

ALLOW 1 hour

START Bowling Green station, 4/5 train

FINISH Bowling Green station, 4/5 train

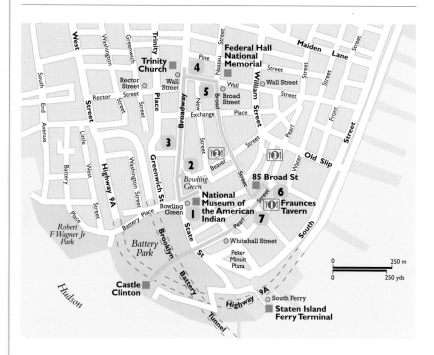

3 Walk north on Broadway to the corner of Wall Street and stop at Trinity Church.

Trinity is the oldest Episcopal Church in the city, and during the 19th century it was the fashionable house of worship for New York's social set. Three churches have graced this spot: a 1698 building that burned down in the American Revolution; a 1790 building felled by a snowstorm; and this Gothic Revival structure by Richard Upjohn,

consecrated in 1846. Also of note are later additions, including the doors by Karl Bitter, based on the baptistery in Florence, and a reredos by Frederick Withers. The churchyard has legible headstones dating back to 1681. The most famous New Yorkers buried here are America's first Treasury Secretary, Alexander Hamilton (in the south yard, under the obelisk) who was felled in a duel with America's Vice President, and Robert Fulton, inventor of the steamship. In the north yard is the man who haunts

the church, comedian Adam Allyn, who died on the way to a gig. His gravestone reminds us that while he 'possessed many good qualit[ie]s', he was a man 'and had the frailties common to man's nature'. At night, he allegedly cackles at passersby.

TRINITY CHURCH; MON–FRI 7–6, SAT–SUN 8–4; TEL: 212-602-0800

4 Walk east two blocks on Wall Street to the intersection with Nassau Street.

The term 'Wall Street' has become synonymous with high finance because of what happens (and happened) on this spot. The building on the north side of Wall Street—marked by a statue of George Washington—is the Federal Hall National Memorial. This 1842 structure replaced the first home of the US government where, on 30 April 1789, George Washington took the oath of office as America's first president. Fifteen months later the capital transferred to Philadelphia, but New York was allowed to keep its role as the country's financial centre, in return for giving up its claim to politics. Soon after, a group of traders met underneath a tree on Wall Street to draw up the terms of what would become the New York Stock Exchange. If you look at the Exchange's current home across Wall Street from Federal Hall, you'll see a scrawny tree planted in front to commemorate the event. This home of the Exchange, built by George B. Post, opened in 1903. It is, unfortunately, considered a top terrorist target, hence the road closures and steel fences. On

the building's pediment stands the giant figure of *Integrity*, her arms outstretched over agriculture and industry. During the Depression, *Integrity* began to crumble, and the sculpture had to be replaced with a cast-iron replica.

5 Walk south on Broad Street (in front of the New York Stock Exchange) two blocks to 85 Broad Street, which is a brown skyscraper surrounded by a covered portico. Follow the portico around to the far side of the building to see the covered archaeological remains.

When this office tower was being constructed in 1979, archaeologists were allowed to dig beneath it to search for one of the most important blocks in old New Amsterdam. Known as the Stadt Huis block, this was home to the first City Hall and many prominent residents. While no trace of the Stadt Huis was uncovered, you can see foundations of a 1670 tavern built by English Governor Francis Lovelace and an old refuse-filled cistern—an archaeologist's dream. Many of the artifacts can be seen on semi-permanent display at the South Street Seaport Museum.

6 Walk along the Pearl Street side of the portico and stop opposite Fraunces Tavern on the corner of Pearl and Broad Streets.

This site once housed Samuel Fraunces' tavern, a centre of revolutionary activity in New York prior to 1776. A favourite spot of George Washington, it was here that he chose to step down as Commander in Chief of the Continental Army in December 1783. The building you are looking at, however, is at best historical conjecture—by the time preservation work began in 1904, little trace of the 18th-century structure remained. Rather than conserve what little was left, architect William Mersereau tore down most of the original building and built this recreation. A small museum details life in early New York.

FRAUNCES TAVERN MUSEUM;
TUE–FRI 12–5, SAT 10–5; TEL: 212-425-1778

7 Cross Broad Street at Pearl Street and walk three blocks west to Battery Park. Pearl Street marks the original shore line and is so-called because Native Americans used it as a dump for oyster shells. From Battery Park, take any path to Castle Clinton.

This fort, built to protect the harbour from British attack during the War of 1812, never saw action. It became a theatre and then, from 1855 to 1889, it was used as the city's first Immigrant Landing Depot, primarily to deal with Irish and German arrivals. When Ellis Island opened, the fort was leased to the New York City Aquarium, which was forced out in 1940 so that the building could be demolished to make way for the Brooklyn-Battery Tunnel. However, conservationists waged a 20-year battle to protect and reconstruct the fort. Eventually, the National Park Service began using it as the ticketing office for people wishing to visit the Statue of Liberty. There is a small museum inside. This is the end of the walk—head north through the park to Bowling Green subway station.

CASTLE CLINTON;
DAILY 8.30–5; TEL: 212-344-7220

CASTLE CLINTON

In the Shadow of the Towers

In a neighbourhood that was once defined primarily by the soaring Twin Towers, encounter history dating back to New York's colonial era.

Before September 11, 2001, the neighbourhood of the World Trade Center was often explored only as an afterthought to visiting the famed 110th-storey observation deck. While today the draw continues to be 'Ground Zero' (as it is known in the media, but almost never called in New York), the streets leading out from the World Trade Center site are rich with architectural and historical gems. These include two other buildings that once claimed the title of tallest in the world; America's oldest continuously used seat of civic government; and New York's oldest church, St Paul's Chapel, which has remarkably escaped fire and devastation time and again over the centuries. The blocks bounded by Liberty Street (south), Vesey Street (north), West Street (west) and Church Street (east) make up the official World Trade Center site, although in fact WTC land extended beyond these boundaries. This is a building site and the directions for the first few stops of the tour may need to be adjusted based on the site's construction. Use common sense and follow the signs on the ground.

Take the E subway to its last stop, World Trade Center, and exit at the front of the train. Follow signs pointing to WTC or World Trade Center. As you leave the subway, you'll pass through windowed doors and then up a brief flight of travertine stairs, which originally led to a shopping arcade and escalators up to the main plaza between Towers 1 and 2 (the 'Twin Towers'). This is the only remaining and publicly accessible section of the original World Trade Center. Walk into the middle of this mezzanine level and exit via the main staircase that leads to Church Street. Cross Church Street at a convenient point so that you can look back at the 16-acre site.

To get a sense of how massive the Twin Towers were, look across the site towards West Street and the World Financial Center. The glass skyscraper with the pyramidal crown (American Express) was built in the 1980s by Cesar Pelli to help soften the World Trade Center's impact on the skyline. It is 55 storeys tall—exactly half the height of Tower 1, which stood directly in front of it.

On the morning of September 11, 2001, two hijacked passenger jets struck the Twin Towers and within hours they had collapsed. With attention focused on the Twin Towers, it's easy to forget the other five WTC buildings—all of which were destroyed, along with a small Greek Orthodox church. In 2007, demolition began on two additional damaged buildings—the former Deutsche Bank Building just to

the south and a university building on nearby West Broadway. The only Trade Center building not on the 16-acre site was WTC 7, and it was quickly replaced. Look north and you will see the replacement, a 52-storey glass skyscraper on Vesey Street, which opened in May 2006. Current construction focuses on three major projects: a massive skyscraper nicknamed the 'Freedom Tower' that will be 1,776ft (541.3m) tall (thus marking 1776, the year of America's independence from Britain); a 4-acre memorial that will encircle and commemorate the footprints of the Twin Towers; and a transit hub designed by Santiago Calatrava.

2 Walk south on Church Street, turning right onto Liberty Street. Walk one block to Greenwich Street.

The fire companies of 'Ten House' were the first on the scene on September 11, only moments after the jet hit Tower 1. The company lost five of its members

DISTANCE 2.15 miles (3.45km)

ALLOW 1.5 hours

START World Trade Center station, E train

FINISH Chambers Street station, J/M/Z trains

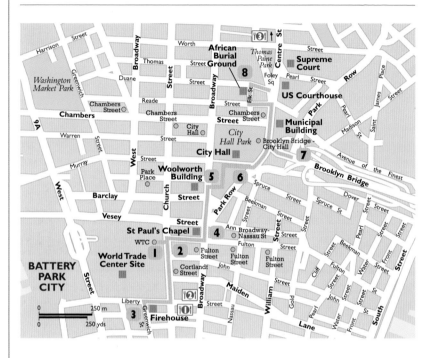

(along with their retired captain, who was Fire and Safety Supervisor at the World Trade Center). Along the west side of the station is a 56ft (17m) bas relief memorial dedicated to the 343 fire personnel who died at the World Trade Center.

3 Retrace your steps to Church Street, turn left and walk three blocks to Fulton Street. Turn right onto Fulton Street, walk one block east to Broadway and enter St Paul's Chapel from the back portico.

The oldest building in continuous use in Manhattan, St Paul's was consecrated in 1766 as a country chapel. Inside, the chapel preserves its plain Georgian interior, including George Washington's private pew used during the brief time New York was America's capital. After the World Trade Center attack the chapel became a place of respite for rescue workers; small displays throughout the building detail this chapter in its history.
ST PAUL'S CHAPEL; MON–FRI 10–6, SAT 8–3, SUN 7–3; TEL: 212-233-4164

height as Park Row, then added a slender tower above, anticipating New York's setback zoning laws by three years.

5 Walk north through City Hall Park to the fence that separates the accessible area of the park from City Hall.

New York's City Hall is the oldest seat of city government still in use in America. Opened in 1812, it was situated so far north of the city that its architects decided it was only worth facing the front and sides in expensive marble—the back was left plain brownstone. When eventually the marble began to deteriorate, the entire building was refitted in limestone. The building currently houses the offices of the Mayor and the City Council chambers; most of the rest of the city government moved to the Municipal Building in 1914. If you look behind and to the east of City Hall you will see the soaring spire of the Municipal Building, crowned by Adolph Weinman's 25ft (7.5m) gold statue of *Civic Fame*.

6 Leave City Hall Park via Park Row and walk north to the entrance of the Brooklyn Bridge. A ten-minute walk takes you out to the Manhattan pier of the bridge.

When the Brooklyn Bridge opened in 1883, Manhattan and Brooklyn were separate cities, with the turbulent East River running between them. At first many assumed a structure held up by

4 Continue walking north on Broadway to Barclay Street, then cross over to the City Hall Park side of the street for the best views of the Woolworth Tower.

Built by Cass Gilbert and finished in 1913, the Woolworth Building was the tallest skyscraper in the world. At the opening gala, the Bishop of New York nicknamed it the 'Cathedral of Commerce', a nod to its gothic styling as well as to New York's preoccupation with wealth. The building is located within sight of the Park Row Building (at 15 Park Row with the twin cupolas), which had been the tallest building in 1899. Gilbert essentially built the base of the Woolworth Building to be the same wire cable would be too fragile to stand, but once it became clear that the bridge was solid, the modern era of steel suspension was born. The bridge also led to the eventual integration—in 1898—of Manhattan and Brooklyn into one large city. Even a short walk out on the bridge offers terrific views of the Financial District skyline, including the Woolworth Tower and WTC 7.

7 Return to Park Row and continue walking north. When you reach Chambers Street (at the Municipal Building), Park Row changes its name to Centre Street. At Reade Street, turn left and walk one short block to Elk Street. Turn right onto Elk Street and continue to the corner of Duane Street.

In this small parcel of land, the graves of 435 black New Yorkers—freedmen and slaves—were uncovered in 1991 during the excavations for a nearby federal office tower. Immediately hailed as one of the city's most important archaeological finds, it shed light on an often forgotten aspect of the city's past. New York did not emancipate its slaves until 1827; in 1800, not long after this graveyard fell out of use, it was the second largest slave-holding city in the US.

8 Walk one block east on Duane Street and then turn right onto Foley Square.

At the centre of Foley Square stands *Triumph of the Human Spirit*, Lorenzo Pace's abstract granite antelope installed

WHERE TO EAT

🍽 TRINITY PLACE,
115 Broadway (entrance on Cedar Street);
Tel: 212-964-0939.
Eat in a gorgeous old bank vault.

🍽 ALAN'S FALAFELS,
in Zuccotti Park (between Church and Broadway); no telephone.
In a city known for 'street food' this is the best. Serves breakfast, too.

🍽 NHA TRANG CENTER,
148 Centre Street (at Walker Street);
Tel: 212-941-9292.
Vietnamese cuisine popular with courthouse staff.

in 2000 to pay tribute to the Africans buried nearby. Across Centre Street from Foley Square stand two of the city's most famous courthouses. The taller, gold-topped building to the south is Cass Gilbert's United States Courthouse, completed by his son in 1936. The smaller building to the north is the 'Supreme Court' (actually a New York County courthouse), completed in 1927 by Guy Lowell. The epigram across the pediment ('The true administration of justice…') is by George Washington. This is the courthouse often seen in movies as diverse as *The Godfather* and *Spiderman 3* and, since 1990, in the television programme *Law & Order*. For the nearest subway, enter the Chambers Street J/M/Z station in Foley Square.

The Jewish Lower East Side

A century ago, this was the largest Jewish neighbourhood in the world, and highlights of its rich past can be found around every corner.

The great wave of Eastern European migration to America in the last two decades of the 19th century brought millions of Jewish settlers to the Lower East Side, making New York the largest Jewish city in the world. The area had once been home to large estates owned by wealthy families. Sold as lots in the late 18th century, the neighbourhood shifted from middle class townhouses to tenements as Irish and German immigrants arrived in the 1840s. By the time Yiddish and Russian-speaking Jews began to displace the earlier immigrants, the Lower East Side had become one of the most densely populated places in history, with thousands of people per acre. While today the Jewish population has shifted to other parts of the city, the neighbourhood retains a flavour of its past. As most Jews living here are Orthodox, all business ceases on Friday afternoons and all day Saturday; if you are planning on visiting any of the shops, do this walk at any other time, including Sunday.

1 Exit the F subway at East Broadway and find a good vantage for 175 East Broadway, the former Jewish Daily Forward Building. Note the Yiddish word *Forverts* spelled out in Hebrew characters at the top.

When the Jewish population reached its peak in the 1920s, nearly 250,000 copies of the *Forward* were published daily, making it one of the largest circulating papers in America. This building, erected in 1912, reveals the paper's political leanings: above the entrance, portrait medallions honour important Communists such as Marx and Engels. Led for years by founding editor Abraham Cahan, the *Forward* was instrumental in America's labour movement, fighting for eight-hour workdays and an end to child labour. This often put Cahan in conflict with other Jewish leaders, including Nathan Straus, for whom this small square is named; Straus was a principal owner of Macy's and a leading capitalist.

2 Walk east on East Broadway to the corner of Jefferson Street.

The building on the south side of the street is the Educational Alliance, a major philanthropic institution. Founded by wealthier German Jews, such as Isidor Straus (Nathan's brother), the Alliance set out to educate Lower East Siders and help them assimilate into American society. Thus, singing lessons weren't just for vocal proficiency, but to teach popular Americans songs. Eddie Cantor, who went on to become one of Hollywood's highest paid actors, took lessons here, as did dance instructor Arthur Murray. Across the street, the Seward Park Library was the most popular branch in the city. It stayed open 19 hours a day and featured the city's largest collection of Yiddish books.

3 Continue walking east on East Broadway to the block on the right between Clinton Street and Montgomery Street.

This is known in Yiddish as 'shteibl row' after the small shopfront synagogues housed here. In a neighbourhood in flux,

DISTANCE 1.65 miles (2.65km)

ALLOW 1 hour

START East Broadway station, F train

FINISH East Broadway station, F train

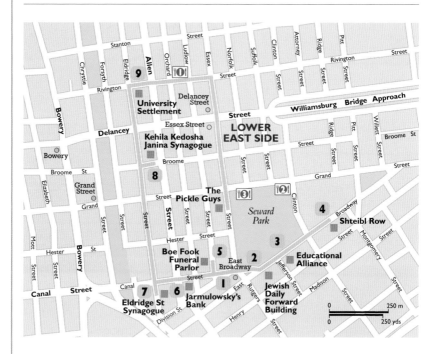

where many immigrants were mixed up and thrown together in new jobs and strange apartments, the synagogues became the primary connections back to the old country and the familiar ways of life. In general, congregations were village- or neighbourhood-based and people worshipped only with others from their original hometown. By the 1920s, this convention led to hundreds of these small synagogues being established in the city's apartments or stores. Today, this row is the only one left.

4 Retrace your steps on East Broadway to Straus Square. Where the road splits, take the Canal Street fork and walk one block west to Ludlow Street, turning right to see the Boe Fook Funeral Parlor on your left.

This building once housed the Kletzker Brotherly Aid Association, founded in 1892. (The date and name can be seen in the pediment.) Just as a synagogue took care of a person's spiritual life, the aid association, or *landsmanschaft* in Yiddish,

took care of secular needs, including job placement, immigrant assistance and banking. This grand building actually housed both, and the faint remains of a Jewish star are still visible in the stucco on the top floor. Like most synagogues, this too was attended by worshippers hailing from the same homeland—Kletzk is located in what is today Belarus. After the *landsmanschaft* sold the building, it became an Italian-Chinese funeral home: Italian clients entered through one door and Chinese through another, even though the funeral arrangements were the same. While this is now fully Chinese, an Italian band still plays at some funeral processions in Chinatown.

5 Return to Canal Street and walk one block west to Orchard Street, where you will find Jarmulowsky's Bank on the southwest corner.

While many people preferred to keep their money with their village-based *landsmanschaft*, there was one highly successful bank, founded by Sender Jarmulowsky in 1873. (You can see

his name engraved above the door.) Jarmulowsky came to the US penniless and sold cloth from a hand basket. He later began reselling passenger ship tickets and reasoned that if people were saving money for these tickets, they might as well do it in a bank. By World War I, thousands of Lower East Side residents had invested millions of dollars in this institution. But when the US entered the war, panicked investors withdrew their funds and the bank failed.

6 Continue west on Canal Street to Eldridge Street. Turn left and walk half a block to the Eldridge Street Synagogue.

The first synagogue built by Eastern European Jews in America, the Eldridge Street Synagogue opened its doors in 1887. The Moorish-Romanesque building is the work of the Herter Brothers, known primarily for their decorative terracotta tenement façades in the neighbourhood. Each element of the façade was encoded with meaning: for example, 12 rosettes in the main

25

Jews, who are a distinct ethnic group and may have descended from Jews enslaved by the Romans in 70 AD. Today, their numbers are dwindling worldwide. The main synagogue in Ionnina, Greece, is shuttered, and this synagogue is the only Romaniote house of worship anywhere in the Western Hemisphere. A small museum inside tells their story, including their terrible plight during the Holocaust.

KEHILA KEDOSHA JANINA SYNAGOGUE; OPEN SUN; TEL: 212-431-1619. www.kkjsm.org

8 Retrace your steps to Eldridge Street, turn right and walk two blocks north, stopping at Rivington Street. The University Settlement is on the southeast corner.

The University Settlement was founded in 1886 to address the needs of immigrant workers and enhance their lives within the community; this was the first social settlement scheme in America. As the name implied, all staff had a formal education, which was not the case with previous missionary workers. Among those who volunteered here was future First Lady Eleanor Roosevelt, who taught dance and calisthenics. This 1898 building is by I.N. Phelps Stokes, who abandoned his budding architectural career to become one of the city's foremost historians.

window representing the 12 tribes of Israel, and the five keyhole windows signifying the Torah. As the size of the congregation diminished, the sanctuary was sealed shut in the 1950s and worship moved to a room in the basement. Since the late 1980s, the non-profit Eldridge Street Project has been doggedly raising funds to preserve and reopen the space. Tours are available on select days when construction permits.

ELDRIDGE STREET SYNAGOGUE; DAYS AND HOURS VARY; TEL: 212-219-0888; www.eldridgestreet.org

7 Return to Canal Street and continue north on Eldridge Street, walking three blocks to Broome Street. Turn right and walk to Kehila Kedosha Janina Synagogue at 280 Broome Street.

While most Jewish immigrants to America were Ashkenazi, New York had a significant population of Romaniote

9 Walk east on Rivington Street four blocks to Essex Street. Turn right and walk three blocks south to arrive at Grand Street.

This block of Essex Street south of Grand is a fine example of the style of tenement apartment dominant between 1879 and 1901. A tenement (the word comes from the Latin 'to hold') generally has four windows across the front; each pair of windows marks the main room of a small 3-room apartment. To get a sense of the size of a typical apartment, visit the Pickle Guys at 49 Essex Street. Their shop, from the entrance to refrigerator, is the size of a typical tenement flat. Pickle shops like this once appeared on most blocks on Lower East Side—before refrigeration, pickling was the best way to preserve most produce. Alan Kaufman and his staff continue to pickle a variety of vegetables and will answer any questions. For the nearest subway, continue down Essex Street to Straus Square.

WHERE TO EAT

🍴 **TEANY,**
90 Rivington Street (between Orchard and Ludlow Streets);
Tel: 212-475-9190.
Musician Moby's veggie tea shop.

🍴 **NOAH'S ARK,**
399 Grand Street (between Clinton and Suffolk Streets);
Tel: 212-674-2200.
Glatt kosher delicatessen.

🍴 **DOUGHNUT PLANT,**
379 Grand Street (at Norfolk Street);
closed Mon;
Tel: 212-505-3700.
Gourmet doughnuts made here.

East Meets West

In New York's bustling immigrant district past and present overlap. Learn about Irish immigration along the streets of America's largest Chinatown.
The parallels between the Irish immigrants who inhabited the streets of Five Points in the 19th century and the Chinese who live on those same streets today are striking. Both populations were largely rural, relatively poor, knew little or no English and adhered to religions seen as strange to many. Despite these obstacles, the Irish prospered in New York, eventually integrating completely into the fabric of American life. Even though there have been Chinese in New York almost as long as there have been Irish, the Chinese are in many ways just starting the process. New York has become the most popular destination for immigrating Chinese and, in the last 40 years, Chinatown has broken away from its past as a tiny neighbourhood into a present where the influence of the Chinese on the rest of the city is beginning to be felt. The busiest time of the week is Sunday afternoon, still reserved by many as market day. To see the neighbourhood at its peak, come then. If you'd prefer more room to walk around, any weekday before 11am will find many of streets empty and the stores just beginning to open.

| Exit the N/Q/R/W, J/M and 6 subway station at Canal Street and walk east along Canal Street to Mulberry Street. Turn right and walk one block to the northeast corner of Bayard Street and the Museum of the Chinese in the Americas.

This 1893 building was once Public School 23, one of the first schools built in an era when social reformers convinced New York of the need to provide adequate public education to immigrant families. The school closed in 1976, just before the museum—then called the New York Chinatown History Project—was founded. This collection relating to Chinese life in America is an excellent introduction not only to New York's Chinatown but to the challenges faced by immigrants throughout the country. (The museum is on the second floor.)
MUSEUM OF THE CHINESE IN THE AMERICAS; TEL: 212-619-4785; www.moca-nyc.org

2 Enter Columbus Park at the southwest corner of Bayard Street and Mulberry Street.

This was once the notorious Mulberry Bend, the part of the Five Points neighbourhood where, after the Civil War, gang violence was at its worst. Journalist, photographer and reformer Jacob Riis documented life in Mulberry Bend (his photo of the alley called 'Bandit's Roost' is still among his most famous), and it was through Riis' efforts that this small park was created.

This is now a hub of the Chinese neighbourhood. At the northern end, near the old pavilion (by Calvert Vaux, co-designer of Central Park), there are often street cobblers and fortune tellers. At the tables, men play *Xiangqi* (Chinese chess). In good weather, men gather at a nearby bird garden with their songbirds. At the southern end of the park are playgrounds and public restrooms.

3 Cross through Columbus Park to its southwest corner.

The neighbourhood was dubbed Five Points in 1829 after the confluence of three streets that came together here to form a five-cornered intersection. Today, only one point remains—the corner of Worth and Baxter Streets. None of the streets bear their original names; Worth and Baxter were renamed after

4

DISTANCE 1.25 miles (2km)

ALLOW 1 hour

START Canal Street station, N/Q/R/W, J/M and 6 trains

FINISH Canal Street station, N/Q/R/W, J/M and 6 trains

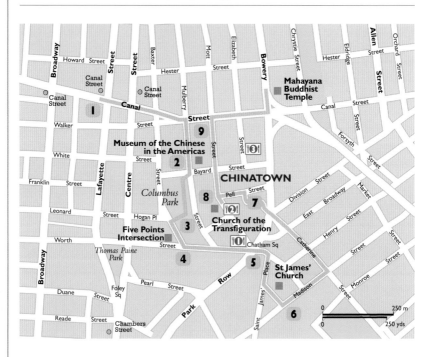

two heroes of the Mexican-American war. The name change was not simply incidental: the city firmly believed it could improve the neighbourhood's fortunes by changing the names of its streets. When that tactic didn't work, it changed their layout, bulldozing houses to extend Worth Street and blocking the extension of Baxter to the south. As a result, when Herbert Asbury wrote the book *Gangs of New York* in 1928 (on which Martin Scorsese's movie was based), he misidentified the actual Five Points, moving it a block east to Mulberry Street.

4 Turn east on Worth Street and walk to the major traffic intersection where Worth meets Mott Street and the Bowery. Here, there is a small park in the centre, with benches.

When the area to the west was Irish Five Points, the neighbourhood spreading east from Chatham Square was reasonably prosperous. Before Worth Street was cut through, the residents here could travel to and from the city via the Bowery and ignore Five Points completely. After the Worth Street extension, this became officially part of the Five Points and is today an integral part of Chinatown. It is also known as Kim Lau Square after the stone memorial arch dedicated to Lt Benjamin Kim Lau and other Chinese-Americans who died in World War II. The statue of Lin Ze Xu commemorates the Fujianese official who tried to keep opium out of China in the 1830s, which ultimately led to the Opium Wars. Most Chinese immigrants coming to New York today are from the Fujian province.

5 Turn right on the east side of Chatham Square onto St James' Place. After passing an old Jewish cemetery, turn left onto James Street, to see St James' Church.

This church, founded in 1827, was constructed sometime in the mid 1830s in an area that was not yet heavily Irish. The first chapter of the Ancient Order of Hibernians was formed here, with the goal of protecting Catholic-owned property from Protestant assault and keeping Catholic children out of the clutches of a public school system that was often full of anti-papist propaganda. (Indeed, where St James' School now stands an anti-Catholic mission set up shop to tempt away the children of parishioners.) Interestingly, James Street got its name long before the church moved in; it is named after a prominent landholder, James DesBrosses.

6 Turn left onto Madison Street and proceed two blocks to Catherine Street. Turn left onto Catherine Street and continue for three blocks. Cross the Bowery to arrive at Doyers Street.

Doyers Street, along with nearby Pell and Mott Streets, formed the heart of the original Chinatown, and gives the best impression today of what the narrow streets were like in the 19th century. This blind curve acquired the name 'bloody angle' during a particularly fierce period of fighting between the On Leong and Hip Sing Tong gangs. By the 1920s, it was said that this was the deadliest spot in America, but that statistic was mostly a product of anti-Chinese sentiment. Today, Doyers Street boasts a host of Chinese barber shops, and patrons travel from far and wide to seek them out.

BLOODY ANGLE

7 Continue on Doyers Street to Pell Street, turn left and walk to Mott Street. Turn left again to the Church of the Transfiguration.

Mott Street was the first street to be settled by the Chinese in New York, many of whom came after the completion of the transcontinental railroad in 1869. To ingratiate themselves into the predominantly Irish neighbourhood, many early Chinese settlers joined the Church of the Transfiguration, easily the most important church in the neighbourhood. Built in 1801 as a Lutheran church, the building was purchased in 1853 by the Catholic diocese to serve the growing Irish population. By the turn of the 20th century, the congregation was almost wholly Italian. Note the plaque to the left of the main entrance that lists the young men from the parish who died in World War I: three are Irish; all the others are Italian. Today, services are held on Sundays in three languages—English, Cantonese and Mandarin.

8 Turn around and head north on Mott Street until you reach No. 65.

This tenement building, built in 1824, is the first purpose-built apartment building ever erected in New York. At seven storeys, it is taller than the average tenement; indeed, builders soon learnt that even the city's poorest residents wouldn't pay rent on an apartment with so many stairs from the street. Note also the unadorned façade. Later buildings

WHERE TO EAT

🍴 **BUDDHA BODAI VEGETARIAN RESTAURANT,**
5 Mott Street; Tel: 212-566-8388.
Buddhist (and kosher) vegetarian fare.

🍴 **SILK ROAD CAFE,**
30 Mott Street; Tel: 212-566-3738.
Western café drinks and eastern specialities like bubble tea.

🍴 **JING FONG,**
20 Elizabeth Street (between Canal and Bayard Streets);
Tel: 212-964-5256.
Hong Kong-style dim sum, with food served from carts at large communal tables.

use decorative stone and terracotta to distinguish themselves; this building, being the first, had no competition.

9 Continue north on Mott Street to Canal Street, then walk two blocks east to the Bowery. The Mahayana Buddhist Temple is at 133 Canal Street.

The largest and most accessible Buddhist temple in Chinatown, the Mahayana temple features a grand golden Buddha (seated on a lotus) that is probably the largest in the city. As in most Buddhist temples, people come throughout the day to light incense, leave offerings and pray. It also serves as a community centre. For the nearest subway, walk west on Canal Street to your starting point.

WALK
5

Little Italy
and NoLita

Explore New York's famous Italian neighbourhood, from the restaurants and shops of Mulberry Street to charming, boutique-filled NoLita.

Visitors to Little Italy are often surprised to find it reduced to just one small street. But while the most visible section of the neighbourhood is Mulberry Street with its shops and restaurants, in fact the Italian community once occupied most of the 50 square blocks north of Canal Street. This walk explores a section of this older Little Italy, including the part now known as NoLita (North of Little Italy), which was an integral part of the old Italian community. Italians began coming to New York after the Civil War as 'birds of passage'— single men working for months at a time and then returning to their families. As America tightened its immigration requirements in the 1880s, men began to stay (and bring over their wives and children), and Little Italy was born. At its peak, over 100,000 people lived on these streets; today, the Italian population is less than a thousand. Streets were often segregated by place of origin: Neapolitans lived on Mulberry Street and Sicilians lived on Elizabeth Street. Indeed, sometimes tenement apartment buildings held people just from one village.

1 Exit the N/Q/R/W, J/M and 6 subway station at Canal Street and walk east on Canal Street to Baxter Street. Turn left for the Church of the Most Precious Blood.

This church, built in the 1890s, quickly became the most important Italian parish in the neighbourhood. Its name refers not only to the blood of Christ, but also to San Gennaro, the patron saint of Naples, whose dried blood, kept in Naples' cathedral, is said to liquefy on his feast day. Today, the biggest event in Little Italy's calendar is the Feast of San Gennaro, a ten-day festival in mid September that runs along Mulberry Street. It features an array of carnival games and Italian food vendors selling their wares. Notice the advertisements flanking the front door for sexton Charles Baciagalupo, the local undertaker.

2 Return to Canal Street and walk one block east to Mulberry Street. Turn left and walk one block until you reach Da Gennaro Restaurant.

In its previous incarnation, this was Umberto's Clam House where, on 7 April 1972, the gangster 'Crazy' Joey Gallo was gunned down on his 43rd birthday. The event, immortalized in Bob Dylan's *Joey*, was the last significant mob hit in Little Italy, though mafia influence didn't wane in the neighbourhood for another 20 years. Umberto's has reopened two blocks north.

DA GENNARO RESTAURANT;
OPEN DAILY; TEL: 212-431-3934

WHERE TO EAT

🍴 FERRARA BAKERY & CAFÉ,
195 Grand Street (between Mulberry and Mott);
Tel: 212-226-6150.
Little Italy's first espresso bar.

🍴 DA NICO,
164 Mulberry Street (between Grand and Broome)
Tel: 212-343-1212.
Southern Italian cuisine in an elegant, relaxed atmosphere.

🍴 LOMBARDI'S,
32 Spring Street (between Mott and Mulberry);
Tel: 212-941-7994
America's first pizzeria and, to many aficionados, still the best.

3 Continue walking one block north on Mulberry Street to Grand Street. The former Banca Stabile is on the southwest corner of the intersection.

Italian for the 'stable bank' (though it was named after its founder, Francesco Stabile), Banca Stabile provided much more than basic financial services. It also sent telegrams and sold passenger ship tickets. Posters in the window still show a number of different steamship lines. This bank has recently been purchased by the Italian American Museum, which plans to renovate and move in by 2010. They will keep much of the original furnishings, including teller windows and a giant safe.

DISTANCE **1.25 miles (2km)**

ALLOW **45 minutes**

START **Canal Street station, N/Q/R/W/, J/M, and 6 trains**

FINISH **Broadway-Lafayette Street station, B/D/F/V trains**

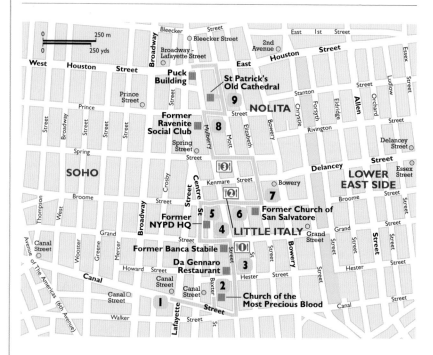

4 Walk two blocks west on Grand Street, then turn right onto Centre Street to look at the former New York Police Department Headquarters.

The unification of New York into five boroughs in 1898 greatly increased the size of city government, which in turn led to a boom in civic building. The Police Department moved from their much smaller quarters on Mulberry Street to this elegant palace in 1909, a building that was designed to 'impress both the officer and the prisoner with the majesty of the law.' Architects Hoppin & Koen modelled it on a host of French buildings, including the Hotel des Invalides in Paris. Flanking the pediment are votaries carrying signs for the Bronx, Brooklyn, Queens and Richmond (the county of Staten Island). Above the pediment, enthroned, is Manhattan, ruling over the others. After a period of disuse when the police moved out in 1973, the building has now been converted into high-priced condominiums.

5 Continue north to Broome Street. Turn right and go two-and-a-half blocks east to 375 Broome Street, best seen from the other side of the street.

Classic tenements, like this one, are five-storey buildings with four front windows. The apartments inside were tiny (usually two or three rooms) and most had access only to a common bathroom in the hall. Since tenants rarely had the opportunity to view an apartment before renting, they relied on a building's exterior decoration as a gauge of the quality inside. This building, designed by the Herter Brothers, is rich in terracotta details. Note the Jewish stars below the top windows; for prospective Jewish tenants this would have been reassuring, but to most Italians the symbol was unknown. And while the head in the pediment's niche is thought by some to be that of Moses, it could also be that of Garibaldi. It is probable that the head became whoever the prospective tenant wanted it to be!

6 Continue one block further east on Broome Street to see the former Church of San Salvatore.

This church, built by Hoppin & Koen at the same time they were constructing the nearby Police Headquarters, was the most majestic in Little Italy. It was also a Protestant Episcopal mission designed to lure Roman Catholics with the promise of a mass in Italian (not Latin). For many, this was a tempting alternative—the closest Catholic churches were heavily Irish and at one point the Pope had to intercede to make sure that Italian parishioners were being treated fairly. When Italians began to leave the neighbourhood after World War II, the space was sold. It is now the Ukrainian Orthodox Cathedral.

7 Turn left onto Elizabeth Street and head north two blocks. Turn left onto Spring Street and, after two blocks, turn right onto Mulberry Street for the former home of the Ravenite Social Club at No. 247. You are now in NoLita.

Until 1998, the ground floor of this tenement housed the Ravenite Social Club, the gathering spot of the Gambino crime family and its most famous *capo* John Gotti. After engineering the murder of Paul Castellano in 1985, Gotti took control of the family's operations; he took to wearing custom-made suits and reveling in his newfound fame as the 'Dapper Don'. (Curious tourists would sometimes be surprised to see him come out of the club to sign autographs and have his photograph taken.) In the late 1980s, the FBI planted microphones in the club, so Gotti and his associates took their conversations upstairs to a vacant apartment—unaware that the FBI had bugged it, too. Gotti was arrested here in 1990 on charges of everything from murder to tax evasion. He died in prison in 2002. When the federal government seized this building in the 1990s, the front was still a sheer wall of brick, put up to try to foul the government's listening devices. All traces of the club are gone except for the old tenement flooring in the current shoe store.

8 Continue on Mulberry Street to Prince Street. Turn right, walk one block and then turn left onto Mott Street, for the entrance to St Patrick's (Old) Cathedral.

Built by Joseph-Francois Mangin (the co-architect of City Hall), this is the oldest Roman Catholic church structure left in the city and its first transitional Gothic building. Dedicated in 1815, it served as the cathedral until 1879. However, in 1866, most of the interior was gutted and the church was rebuilt with the current brownstone front and new columns made out of cast iron (which was valued not just for its strength, but also for its fireproof qualities). The high wall surrounding the churchyard proved beneficial for protecting Irish immigrants from periodic outbreaks of Protestant-led violence. Among those buried here is the Venerable Pierre Toussaint, the Haitian-born slave who is currently being considered for sainthood.

9 Continue north to East Houston Street. Turn left and walk one block for the Puck Building.

The satirical magazine *Puck* was first published here in 1887, two years after the building's completion. The magazine only lasted until 1916, but was vastly popular in its day—in particular because of its criticisms of New York's political machine. Some think that the city's decision to widen Houston Street was in part out of annoyance at the jibes levelled at it in the pages of *Puck*. The building lost a portion of its annexe and had to move its entrance to Lafayette Street. Above the entrance, as well as on the corner of Mulberry Street, stand gold statues of Puck. The Layfayette Street B/D/F/V subway is across the street.

SoHo and TriBeCa

In 150 years, these two neighbourhoods have gone in and out of fashion, with factories and warehouses becoming the city's trendiest real estate.

SoHo (the blocks South of Houston Street) and TriBeCa (the Triangle Below Canal Street) are modern names for neighbourhoods that first flourished during the industrial boom in the mid 19th century. Broadway north of Canal Street became the city's first luxury shopping street, while TriBeCa's warehouses served the burgeoning Hudson River docks. Builders turned to prefabricated cast iron to create false fronts on buildings, which allowed merchants to build grand stores at a fraction of the cost. Today, SoHo and TriBeCa contain the best cast-iron façades in the world. As commerce moved uptown and manufacturing left New York, the buildings were slowly abandoned and it seemed in the 1940s and 50s that the area might collapse from neglect. Enter the artists, who found the open manufacturing spaces to be ideal for creating large-scale modern art. Today, the area has returned to its former glory, with loft apartments and up-market shops that are less crowded early on weekday mornings. The place really comes alive on weekend afternoons.

Exit the N/Q/R/W, J/M and 6 subway station at Canal Street and Broadway and walk north on Broadway three blocks, stopping at Broome Street where you will see a cast-iron building on the northeast corner.

The grandest of all cast-iron buildings, this ornate Palladian dry goods store was originally built by china merchant E. V. Haughwout in 1857. Haughwout's merchandise was renowned (he supplied porcelain to the White House), but the store became world-famous as the first building where cast iron was used as a structural support, rather than purely decoratively. In addition, Haughwout was the first American to install a commercial passenger elevator, just four years after Elisha Otis publicly demonstrated the efficacy of the safety brake. The elevator was steam driven (you can still see the wooden water tank at the rear) and was instantly popular. Together, the metal frame and elevator make this the proto-skyscraper and the most architecturally advanced structure of its day.

2 Continue north on Broadway two blocks to Prince Street and turn left. Stop halfway down the first block.

Ernest Flagg built this L-shaped manufacturing and office space for the Singer (sewing machine) Manufacturing Company in 1904, at the tail end of the cast-iron era. Flagg's dramatic green and red building bucked the trend of most metal constructions, which were painted to resemble stone. Just two years

WHERE TO EAT

[◯] FANELLI'S,
94 Prince Street (at Mercer);
Tel: 212-226-9412.
Classic old New York Irish pub.

[◯] LE PETIT CAFÉ,
156 Spring Street (between
West Broadway & Wooster);
Tel: 212-219-9723.
Busy neighbourhood coffee shop,
often filled with shoppers.

[◯] BUBBY'S,
120 Hudson Street
(at North Moore);
Tel: 212-219-0666.
American bistro known for its
delectable pie.

later, Flagg completed another building for Singer using the same bold colour scheme; this skyscraper in the Financial District (now gone) was briefly the world's tallest building.

3 Continue to walk west, stopping at 99 Prince Street.

The basements of most SoHo buildings extend well beyond the street frontage to provide extra storage space. When these buildings were constructed, lighting these dank basements with kerosene or weak electric bulbs was insufficient, so an innovative system of circular glass tiles was installed to flood the basements with natural light. This is one of the

DISTANCE 1.75 miles (2.8km)

ALLOW 1 hour

START Canal Street station, N/Q/R/W, J/M and 6 trains

FINISH Franklin Street station, 1 train

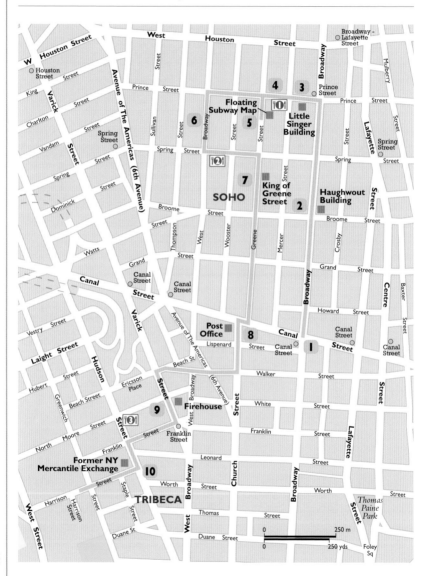

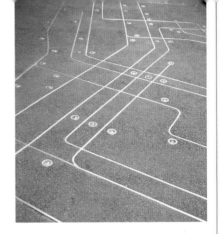

best-preserved examples—note the tiles in the stairs as well as the pavement. On many other pavements, the glass has been replaced with sheets of metal.

4 Continue on Prince Street to Greene Street, then turn left and walk to 110 Greene Street.

In 1986, artist Françoise Schein took typical 19th-century sidewalk glass and turned it into this 'Floating Subway Map'. Starting in the 1950s, SoHo became the city's most vibrant artistic neighbourhood, with painters and sculptors given preferential zoning to restore old manufacturing buildings. A plethora of galleries soon followed, particularly along Broadway and West Broadway. Today, many artists have found the escalating rents prohibitive and have left Manhattan altogether, while the galleries are predominantly now in Chelsea. Look across the street, back towards the corner of Prince Street, to see Richard Hass' 1974 *trompe l'oeil* painting of a cast-iron façade, complete with cats in a lower window.

5 Return to Prince Street, turn left and walk two blocks west to West Broadway. Turn left and head south half a block to 422 West Broadway.

New York street names often reveal the changing fortunes of a neighbourhood. West Broadway was originally Laurens Street, but the gradual shift of commerce uptown led civic boosters to rename it 'South Fifth Avenue', in an attempt to

link uptown elegance to a downtown street. Building lots were renumbered in an unusual fashion, beginning at Washington Square Park and heading downtown. Thus, still cast into the metal columns of this 1873 storefront is its old South Fifth Avenue address, '130'. The scheme was confusing and unpopular and the street was changed again—to West Broadway—in 1896.

6 Continue south to Spring Street and turn left. Walk two blocks back to Greene Street and turn right. Halfway down the block is 72-76 Greene Street.

Known as the 'King of Greene Street', this is perhaps the best example of a cast-iron building on a street of consistently great structures. It was built by architect Isaac Duckworth in 1873 for merchant Gardner Colby, whose fortune later endowed Maine's Colby College. While some SoHo buildings were designed by world-renowned architects, most were the work of men like Duckworth, who specialized in cast iron. Recently restored and repainted, this building gives a good

45

idea of what all of SoHo looked like in its heyday. However, just 20 years prior to this building's completion, Greene Street wasn't even considered part of the shopping district. Indeed, an 1859 guide to high-class New York brothels notes the particularly attentive service at 76 Greene.

7 Continue south on Greene Street two-and-a-half blocks to Canal Street. Cross Canal to the corner of Church Street. Having crossed Canal Street, you are now officially in TriBeCa. In front of you is the post office.

This 1939 Art Moderne post office is a rare building from that period to be found in this part of the city. Inside, Wheeler Williams' grand bas relief of a Native American hunter—which wouldn't look out of place at the Rockefeller Center—graces the lobby.

8 Walk two blocks south on Church Street to Walker Street. Turn right and walk three short blocks west to Varick Street. Turn left and walk one block to North Moore Street. The fire station is on the southeast corner.

At the turn of the 20th century, New York embarked on a plan to rebuild its civic structures, including all firehouses. This example, from 1912, is best known as the headquarters of the *Ghostbusters* in the film of the same name.

9 Continue south on Varick Street to Franklin Street, then turn right and walk one block to Hudson Street. Turn left and walk to the corner of Hudson Street and Harrison Street where you can see the Mercantile Exchange.

The expansion of commodities markets in New York in the latter part of the 19th century led to the creation of a Butter and Cheese Exchange, reborn in 1882 as the New York Mercantile Exchange. Architect Thomas R. Jackson built this impressive trading floor from 1884–86 in the heart of the fresh produce district, then known as the Lower West Side. At its peak, it's said that over $15,000 in eggs traded here every hour.

10 Walk one block west on Harrison Street to Greenwich Street. You'll pass tiny Staple Street, perhaps gaining its name from the staples (bread, cheese, eggs, etc.) traded at the Mercantile Exchange. Cross Greenwich Street.

Nestled into the campus of Manhattan Community College is a row of Federal homes, many of which were moved here from nearby Washington Street during the college's construction. Some are by John McComb, Jr, co-architect of City Hall; 27 Harrison Street was his own home. These houses are a reminder that this was once a well-to-do residential area, with some industry along the waterfront. As Manhattan's port expanded up the Hudson, most homes were torn down in favour of larger warehouse, factory and produce-storage buildings. For the subway, retrace your steps to the Franklin Street station and the 1 train.

COOPER UNION

NoHo and the Notorious Bowery

Notice the contrasts in an area where Lafayette Street, once one of Manhattan's best addresses, ran next to one of its worst, the Bowery.

John Jacob Astor was already wealthy when he began investing in Manhattan real estate; by the time he died in 1848 he was America's richest man (and supposedly said on his deathbed, "If only I'd bought more.") One of his first shrewd property developments was the creation of Lafayette Street, opened in 1825 by the Marquis himself. However, over the next few decades the area went from expensive elegance to industrialization and—in particular on the Bowery—became one of the poorest parts of town. By the end of the 19th century, the song *The Bowery* made it fashionable to sing, "I'll never go there any more!" when, in fact, tourists and New Yorkers were fascinated with 'skid row', and the Bowery bums who inhabited it. Today, the neighbourhood is experiencing rapid gentrification. The term NoHo (North of Houston) came into vogue in the 1980s, as artists who had been forced out of SoHo by skyrocketing prices found cheaper rents in the old factories and warehouses. Still an area in transition, NoHo has fluid borders and an even more fluid personality, and the character of the streets seems to change with every block.

1 Exit the 6 Astor Place subway station and walk to *The Alamo* (the big black cube) in the middle of Astor Place.

Tony Rosenthal created *The Alamo* in 1966 as part of the city's temporary exhibition, 'Sculpture in Environment'. The name was suggested by his wife, for whom the impenetrability of the work reminded her of the fortress in San Antonio. At the request of students of nearby Cooper Union, the city acquired the work in 1967, making it the first piece of abstract sculpture in the city's permanent collection. The work is designed to rotate on its axis, so feel free to go up and give it a spin.

2 Look across the street at Cooper Union.

Peter Cooper was one of the most successful New Yorkers of his age. He was inventor of the *Tom Thumb*, the first American-made, steam locomotive; he was a principal in the company that laid the first transatlantic telegraph cable—he even patented edible gelatine. Cooper achieved all this without the benefit of a college education, as he was too poor to attend university. To help other clever-but-impoverished students, he created the Cooper Union for the Advancement of Science and Art in 1859 and ran it as a completely free-tuition institution, which it remains to this day. The building's ground floor features the Great Hall, the largest indoor public space at that time. It was here in 1860 that Abraham Lincoln gave his 'Right Makes Might' speech,

an oration that he later credited with winning him the presidency.

3 Walk in front of Cooper Union to Third Avenue. Turn right and walk one block to 7th Street, then turn left and proceed half a block to McSorley's Old Ale House.

While some historians quibble with the 1854 opening date, McSorley's is clearly the oldest continuously operating tavern in New York. It is the only one that didn't have to close during Prohibition. They have only ever served one thing—their own ale, in light and dark varieties—and during Prohibition they officially served a watered-down brew, while they were still concocting the real stuff in the basement. The walls are decorated with memorabilia from the bar's long history, including a rare 'Wanted' poster for John Wilkes Booth, assassin of Abraham

DISTANCE 1.15 miles (1.85km)

ALLOW 45 minutes (longer with museum visit)

START Astor Place station, 6 train

FINISH Astor Place station, 6 train

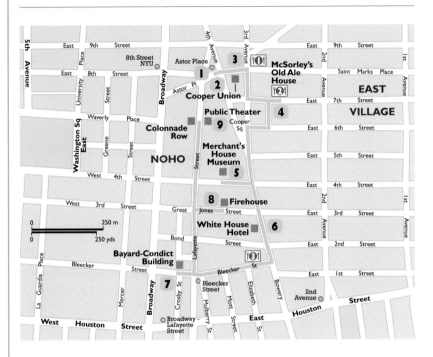

Lincoln. Originally, the bar was men-only—their motto was 'Good Ale, Raw Onions and No Ladies'. But in 1970 a lawsuit opened the doors to female patronage and they are welcomed warmly today.

MCSORLEY'S OLD ALE HOUSE;
MON–SAT 11AM–1AM, SUN 1PM–1AM;
TEL: 212-474-9148

4 Leave 7th Street via Taras Shevchenko Place. Turn right onto 6th Street and left onto the Bowery.

Walk two blocks, turn right and go to the Merchant's House Museum at 29 East 4th Street.

This home, built in 1832, was purchased by merchant Seabury Tredwell in 1835 and his family continued to live here for the next 98 years. Daughter Gertrude was born here and died in the house in 1933; three years later, it opened as a museum, completely preserved as Gertrude had kept it—with many of her parents' original furnishings! This is also one of

men could rent a bed for just a few cents a night. (At some, they slept in shifts, each person renting the bed for just eight hours.) Only a few flop houses, such as the White House, remain amidst the new condos that are coming to define NoHo.

6 Continue south on the Bowery to Bleecker Street. Turn right and walk five-and-a-half small blocks to 65 Bleecker Street, which is opposite Crosby Street. This is the site of the Bayard-Condict Building.

This 1899 building is the only Louis Sullivan skyscraper in New York and, as such, would be important even if it wasn't such a gorgeous building. Sullivan is famous for his dictum 'form ever follows function', which hard-line modernists took to mean that all non-functional ornamentation was therefore superfluous. This building disproves that reading, for Sullivan has used decorative terracotta to great effect here, including on the underside of the cornice. Sullivan's other trademark—making buildings look taller than they truly were—is also amply demonstrated. Floor heights decrease as the building goes up, so that, due to a trick of perspective, the building appears considerably taller than it actually is. To accentuate this effect, Sullivan includes unbroken mullions that rise from the second floor up to the giant angels that stand beneath the cornice.

the most reliably haunted houses in the city, with sightings of Gertrude having been made countless times over the last 70 years. In a city that has often valued progress over preservation, to have a townhouse like this intact is a remarkable boon, and anyone interested in the period is encouraged to visit.

MERCHANT'S HOUSE MUSEUM;
THU–MON AFTERNOONS ONLY;
TEL: 212-777-1089; www.merchantshouse.com

5 Return to the Bowery and turn right. Walk south to 340 Bowery for the White House Hotel.

For years, the word 'Bowery' was always accompanied by the word 'bum'. In the middle of the 19th century, the street began to teem with 'flop houses' where

7 Retrace your steps to Lafayette Street. Turn left and proceed two blocks north, turning right onto Great

Jones Street. Go to Engine Company
No. 33 at 44 Great Jones Street.

In the wake of five-borough unification
in 1898, New York began an ambitious
plan to rebuild its fire stations in grand
Beaux Arts style. This coincided with
a 30-year effort by the city to replace
its corrupt volunteer fire department
with professional companies, a move
symbolized by the lavish attention paid to
the professional company's houses. This
splendid example is by Ernest Flagg.

8 Retrace your steps to Lafayette
Street. Turn right and walk one-and-
a-half blocks to Colonnade Row, on the
west side of the street.

Formally known as La Grange Terrace,
this was the centre of John Jacob Astor's
real estate development along newly
created Lafayette Street. Nine homes
opened in 1833, all made of marble
with a stunning two-storey colonnade
running the length of the building. Astor
resided here at the end of his life, as did
a number of other wealthy merchants,
including Franklin Delano, grandfather
of President Roosevelt. Today, only four
homes remain, their worn façades only a
pale semblance of their original glory.

9 Opposite Colonnade Row, on the
east side of the street, you will see
the Public Theater.

When John Jacob Astor died in 1848, he
left $400,000 for the establishment of a
research library. This building opened

WHERE TO EAT

🍴 CHICKPEA,
23 Third Avenue (between
St Marks and 9th Street);
Tel: 212-254-9500.
Middle Eastern falafel joint.

🍴 McSORLEY'S OLD ALE HOUSE,
15 East 7th Street;
Tel: 212-474-9148.
Order a 'one and one' of their ale.

🍴 QUARTINO,
11 Bleecker Street (between
Lafayette and the Bowery);
Tel: 212-529-5133.
Organic Italian specialities.

in 1854 and additions expanded it to
its present size in 1869 and 1881. The
original trustees included Washington
Irving and Joseph Cogswell; they decided
on a closed-stack reference library since
no one wanted to see 'a crowd ranging
lawlessly among the books.' (Cogswell
also later lamented that the 'young fry'
wasted their time in the library reading
trash like Charles Dickens.) When the
Astor Library was folded into the newly
created New York Public Library at the
end of the 19th century, the building
became the Hebrew Immigrant Aid
Society. In 1967, the Public Theater
opened in the space with the première of
Hair. There are now seven theatres here.
For the nearest subway, continue walking
north on Lafayette Street and return to
the Astor Place station.

Gilded Age Greenwich Village

Visit the area around charming Washington Square and see some of the best-preserved examples of the city as it was in the late 19th century.

Until the 1820s, New York's northern border barely extended north of Chambers Street. But a yellow fever epidemic in 1822 caused the wealthy to flee, and within a decade Washington Square was considered the best address in the city. The neighbourhood prospered throughout the 19th century and even as the wealthiest New Yorkers edged up Fifth Avenue towards Central Park, Greenwich Village stayed a genteel neighbourhood. As the city entered its Gilded Age (roughly 1870-1910), the Village forged the identity that would make it synonymous with Bohemianism in the 20th century—artists and writers mingling with wealthy merchants and immigrant factory workers in a district that became a flourishing microcosm of the city as a whole. The Village (as all New Yorkers call it) is active every day of the week, but Washington Square reaches a peak on weekend afternoons. The Church of the Ascension is worth seeing inside and is usually open Monday-Saturday, noon-1pm, but check in advance. This tour is the companion to 'Off the Grid in the West Village'; each starts in a different location, but ends at the same place.

1 Exit the R/W subway at 8th Street. Walk south on Broadway to Waverly Place, then turn right and walk three blocks to Washington Square.

In the 18th century, Washington Square was the city burial ground for poor or unknown people, and it is estimated that more than 20,000 people—mostly victims of epidemics—are still buried beneath its dirt and asphalt. However, as the population of the Village soared after 1822 (when yellow fever quarantined lower Manhattan), the city hatched a plan to elevate property values by paving over the graveyard. On 4 July 1826, the new Washington Square was born, first as a military parade ground, and then as a formal park. The central fountain is a popular performance venue and on a sunny day you will see scores of musicians dotted about in the park.

2 Leave the east side of the park on Washington Place and walk one block east to reach the corner of Greene Street.

Even as other parts of Greenwich Village stayed prosperous during the latter part of the 19th century, the area between the park's eastern flank and the Bowery became an extension of SoHo's manufacturing district. The Brown Building—now New York University classrooms—was the home of the notorious Triangle Shirtwaist Factory, long considered one of the worst sweatshops in the city. On 25 March 1911, a fire broke out here, killing 146

young women working the Saturday shift. Most of them had been locked onto the factory floor to minimize unauthorized breaks. When they fled out of the windows, the flimsy fire escapes collapsed beneath their weight. This tragedy—still one of the worst industrial fires in American history—spurred a host of legislation to ensure worker safety, though the owners of the factory got off with only minor fines.

3 Return to Washington Square Park and walk along to the park's northern edge, stopping opposite 7 Washington Square North.

This lovely Greek Revival terrace—known as 'The Row'—is among the city's most important landmarks, for it was the first such row developed to unified aesthetic principles. When

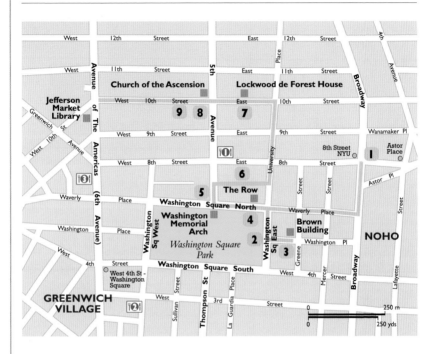

8

DISTANCE **1.25 miles (2km)**

ALLOW **45 minutes**

START **8th Street station, R/W trains**

FINISH **West 4th Street station, A/C/E, B/D/F/V trains**

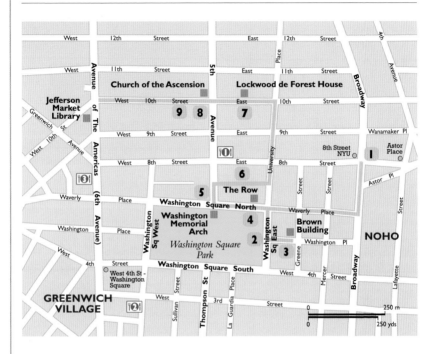

opened in 1832, these were the finest homes in the city. By the Gilded Age, residents were still wealthy but lacked their predecessors' status. In 1880, Village native Henry James published the novella *Washington Square*, still one of the best accounts of the mores of the era. In 1882, novelist Edith Wharton moved into 7 Washington Square North, and Wharton's later books often feature Washington Square. As the wealthy left and buildings were divided into rental apartments, more artists and writers moved in. Most

notably, painter Edward Hopper lived for decades in 3 Washington Square. Most of The Row is now a unified apartment building owned by NYU.

4 Continue west along The Row to the grand arch at the intersection of Fifth Avenue.

One hallmark of the Gilded Age was the City Beautiful movement. Sometimes referred to as Beaux Arts, after the school in Paris, this period in New

OPPOSITE: THE WASHINGTON MEMORIAL ARCH

LOCKWOOD DE FOREST HOUSE

York architecture saw the wholesale creation of buildings that would not look out of place in any European city. This graceful arch can be seen as New York's version of the *arc de triomphe*. The arch, by Stanford White, was dedicated in 1895 but for its first two decades the statue bases stood empty, the result of a fiercely contested argument about what should be depicted—statues representing Washington's virtues or the man himself. Finally, in 1916, the statue of the general ('Washington at War') was added to the left flank of the arch and two years later the statue of the president ('Washington at Peace') was added on the right.

5 Walk north half a block to Washington Mews and turn right into this small alley. Ignore the signs that say 'Private Street'—this is a public pedestrian thoroughfare.

Part of what made the homes of The Row so attractive to the wealthy was this mews—an oddity in early 19th-century New York, where rich and poor lived cheek by jowl in small lots in the overcrowded city. Indeed, so few New Yorkers owned any form of private transport that when the 1811 grid plan of the city was published there were no driveways or rear alleys; builders didn't want to waste the space for a population that would probably never own carriages. These stables are now all private homes. The street here is paved in Belgian Block cobblestone, which originally came to America as ship's ballast. Note how the street cants to the centre where its gutter has been filled in; this is the hallmark of a street paved before 1842 and a real rarity in New York.

6 Walk straight through Washington Mews to University Place. Turn left and walk two-and-a-half blocks to 10th Street. Turn left again and walk to 7 East 10th Street.

This extraordinary home was built by Lockwood de Forest who, along with Louis Comfort Tiffany, founded America's first professional interior design firm. The immense oriel window is Burmese teak, hand carved by de Forest's army of workers in India and installed in 1887. The building next door, built at the same time, was also decorated by de Forest.

7 Continue west to Fifth Avenue and stop at the Church of the Ascension on the corner.

Built in 1840 by Richard Upjohn, this church marked a general rejection of earlier puritan fashions for a more distinctly English Gothic style. Originally plain on the interior, the church was refitted in the 1880s by Stanford White and a team of artists, including Louis Saint-Gaudens, who did the carved angels, and John LaFarge, who created many of the stained-glass windows and the immense altar painting of Christ ascending. This is one of the most glorious church interiors in the city and well worth seeing. This was also the site of the first marriage of a sitting US President, when John Tyler married debutante Julia Gardiner in 1844.

CHURCH OF THE ASCENSION;
TEL: 212-254-8620

8 Continue west to 11 West 10th Street. From here you have a good view of the townhouses on the opposite side of the street.

This block of West 10th Street was the first in the city to be dominated by artists. Mark Twain lived at No. 14, and Emma Lazarus (whose poem 'The New Colossus' raised funds for the Statue of Liberty) resided at No. 18; moreover, the whole attached terrace from 20–38 was built specifically as artists' apartments. At various times Marcel Duchamp, Leonard Bernstein, Khalil Gibran and Dashiell Hammett all called this home. The nearby (and now-demolished) 10th Street Studio, built by Richard Morris Hunt, was home to such painters as William Merritt Chase, John Sloan and Winslow Homer.

WHERE TO EAT

🍴 **OTTO ENOTECA AND PIZZERIA, One Fifth Avenue (entrance on 8th Street);**
Tel: 212-995-9559.
Chef Mario Batali's casual pizzeria.

🍴 **CAFFE REGGIO,**
119 MacDougal Street (between Minetta Lane and West 3rd Street);
Tel: 212-475-9557.
Classic Village café and the first cappuccino purveyors in NYC.

🍴 **GOBO,**
401 Sixth Avenue
(between Waverly and 8th Street);
Tel: 212-255-3242.
Vegetarian Pacific Rim specialities; impressive wine list.

9 Continue west on 10th Street to the corner of Sixth Avenue.

This ornate Victorian Gothic building was originally a courthouse, despite its ecclesiastic style. Architect Frederick Withers even included a tympanum above the main entry. However, instead of Christ as the central figure, Withers picked the judge from *The Merchant of Venice*. If you look closely, you can see the figure next to the judge is Shylock, a scale in one hand and knife in the other, ready to take his pound of flesh. To reach the nearest subway, walk south down Sixth Avenue until you reach the West 4th Street station.

WASHINGTON MEWS

Off the Grid in the West Village

Discover architectural gems along the byways of old Greenwich Village, including gardens, homes and speakeasies from the Roaring Twenties.

When the city published the Commissioners' Plan in 1811—which laid out the regular grid of streets north of Houston Street—everything in Greenwich Village west of Sixth Avenue was conspicuously left out. The large estate owners didn't want the city cutting up their properties and lobbied effectively for exclusion. When the population of the area boomed after an 1822 yellow fever epidemic downtown, those same landowners subdivided their properties into house lots and created frontage by squeezing new streets into the preexisting village roads. The result is a neighbourhood where Manhattan's usually rigid logic gives way to meandering streets and sometimes confusing interchanges and street names. (Although we don't visit it on this tour, this is the part of town where 4th Street and 10th Street—supposedly six blocks apart—cross each other.) This walk is the companion to 'Gilded Age Greenwich Village,' which starts in a different location, but ends at the same place.

1 Exit the 1 subway at Christopher Street. Walk west on Christopher Street, away from Christopher Park, a few short blocks to Hudson Street and turn left. Continue to the Church of St Luke in the Fields, where Grove Street meets Hudson Street.

When Greenwich Village was actually a village, its hub was Hudson Street, just one block east of the river. (Today, landfill has pushed the banks of the Hudson three blocks further away.) This country chapel was erected in 1821—a year before the Village's population surge—on land originally owned by Trinity Church, Wall Street. Built to serve a rural population, its plain brick façade is a rarity in a city of stone churches.

2 Walk east on Grove Street half a block until you reach the bend in the road. Grove Court is on the right.

The slight angle of Grove Street reveals the junction between two pieces of old Village property, and behind the main houses sits Grove Court, opened in 1854. Grove Court was quickly dubbed 'Mixed Ale Alley' because its poor residents were considered the dregs of society. At the time, passersby knew they were poor simply because their houses did not have street frontage. In a city concerned with wealth and status, showing off one's home—at least the façade—was considered of the utmost importance. Today, the peace and quiet of Grove Court makes it coveted real estate.

WHERE TO EAT

🍴 **PINK TEA CUP,**
42 Grove Street
(between Bedford and Bleecker);
Tel: 212-807-6755.
Sensational soul food; great for brunch.

🍴 **MOUSTACHE,**
90 Bedford Street
(between Grove & Barrow);
Tel: 212-229-2220.
Eclectic Middle Eastern fare, including innovative pita pizzas.

🍴 **JOE: THE ART OF COFFEE,**
141 Waverly Place
(between Gay and Sixth Avenue);
Tel: 212-924-6750.
Popular and often crowded.

3 Continue east on Grove Street to the corner of Bedford Street.

On the northeast corner of this intersection is the most significant wood-frame house in the Village. It was built by William Hyde—a window-sash maker—in 1822 to advertise his skills. Behind it sits 'Twin Peaks', an eclectic mock Tudor-meets-Swiss chalet creation of the 1920s, supposedly to inspire the writers and artists who were flocking to the Village at the time.

4 Turn right onto Bedford Street and walk half a block to No. 86.

OPPOSITE: CHRISTOPHER PARK

65

DISTANCE I mile (1.6km)

ALLOW 45 minutes

START Christopher Street station, I train

FINISH West 4th Street Station, A/C/E, B/D/F/V trains

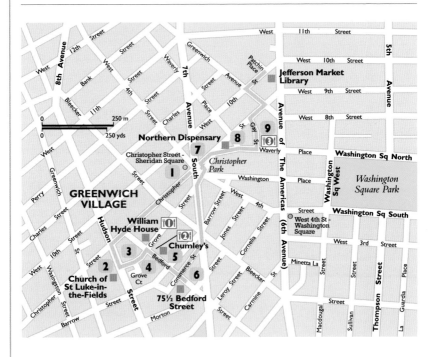

During Prohibition (1920-33), when the sale of alcohol was banned in the United States, the warren of streets in Greenwich Village became the perfect spot to open illegal taverns—or 'speakeasies' as they were commonly known. Chumley's, behind the door at 86 Bedford Street, is a classic example. To those in the know, this door opened into one of the city's literary hotspots. To the uninitiated, however, this looked like nothing more than a plain, old house. Inside the door, patrons were immediately greeted with a steep flight of steps—a barricade designed to slow down raiding federal Prohibition inspectors. From the 1920s to the 1950s, Chumley's played host to writers such as Ernest Hemingway, F. Scott Fitzgerald, Edna St Vincent Millay, Dylan Thomas, Simone de Beauvoir, Allen Ginsberg and scores of others who came to soak up the literary ambience. The American slang expression to 'eighty-six' something—i.e., get rid of it—is said to have come from the address of Chumley's; if the police raided, patrons escaped out the door at 86 Bedford.

However, the expression is restaurant slang that predates the establishment of this bar, and while it may have been popularized here it wasn't coined here.

5 Continue on Bedford Street to stand opposite No. 75½.

This 9½ft (2.9m) wide home, the narrowest in the city, was built in the 1870s into the carriage drive of 77 Bedford (which dates to 1799 and is the oldest home in the neighbourhood). Poet Edna St Vincent Millay lived in this narrow structure in the 1920s immediately after she'd won the Pulitzer Prize. Later, cartoonist William Steig, his wife and his sister-in-law, anthropologist Margaret Mead, called this home. Rumours persist that Cary Grant lived here too, but there's no hard evidence.

6 Walk back on Bedford Street and turn right onto charming Commerce Street. Walk one block to Seventh Avenue South. Turn left and walk back to where you left the subway. Enter Christopher Park.

This small park became a focal point of the neighbourhood in the 1920s with the opening of the subway nearby. (Confusingly, most people refer to this as Sheridan Square—you'll see a statue of General Sheridan in the garden—but his square is actually around the corner.) From the park, find a place where you can see the Stonewall Inn at 53 Christopher Street, which is the birthplace of gay rights in America. A riot broke out here on 27 June 1969, after the police raided the bar, ostensibly to investigate liquor law violations, but really to hassle its gay patrons. There is some debate as to how big a factor this was in causing the riot, but 27 June was also the day of gay icon Judy Garland's funeral, so emotions in the bar were already running high. A year of political action led to the first Gay Pride parade on the Stonewall riot's one-year anniversary. This annual event is now one of New York's largest. The park's bronze statues (with white patina) are the Gay Liberation monument by George Segal, which depict a standing male couple and a seated female couple (see page 64).

7 Facing General Sheridan, leave Christopher Park, from either side exit and walk to the park's narrow point. You will see a triangular brick building labelled 'Northern Dispensary'.

This odd lot is a good example of the problem with the West Village street plan. Each landowner created his own streets—usually with some logic—but when they intersected a neighbour's streets, chaos often followed. The city acquired this land in 1827 to build a free clinic for the Village's working classes residents. Many Village writers relied on the Northern Dispensary over the years; the earliest was Edgar Allan Poe, who in 1836 lived nearby with his new wife—also his first cousin—14-year-old Virginia Clemm.

8 Take a right on Waverly Place, walking in front of the Northern

Dispensary. Notice when you get to the far side that the street coming in from the left is also Waverly Place, a confusing reminder of the haphazard nature of the roads in the neighbourhood. Continue one more short block to Gay Street and turn left to arrive at 12 Gay Street.

The homes along the west side of block-long Gay Street epitomize the type of small residence built by merchants in the 1820s. Later divided into apartments, they housed a variety of artists in the 20th century. Residents of No. 12 included Frank Paris (creator of Howdy Doody), novelist Walter Gibson and showgirl Betty Compton, better known as the mistress of New York's mayor, Jimmy Walker.

9 Continue on Gay Street to Christopher Street. Turn right, walk one block to Greenwich Avenue, then turn left and walk to 10th Street. Turn right and walk half a block to the alley of Patchin Place on your left.

Like Grove Court, these small, off-street buildings housed lower-income residents (originally workers from a nearby hotel). Among those who called this home were poet e.e. cummings and revolutionary John Reed, who began work on *Ten Days That Shook the World* here. (Reed is the only American to be buried in the Kremlin.) This was also Marlon Brando's first New York City home. The old lamp at the alley's far end is the only original gas lamp left in Manhattan, although it is now electrified. For the nearest subway, continue on 10th Street, then turn right onto Sixth Avenue and walk to the A/C/E and B/D/F/V West 4th Street station.

From Prussians to Punks

The East Village encompasses everything from country gentility to a squatters' riot, from German immigrants to the Hell's Angels.

The term East Village was created after World War II to convince renters that they were moving into an area which had more in common with genteel Greenwich Village than with the teeming Lower East Side, to which these streets were once considered integral. This area had been part of Dutch Governor Peter Stuyvesant's farm and the land was initially developed by the family for upper middle-class tenants. The large numbers of German immigrants coming into the city after 1848 changed the neighbourhood's character and for the rest of the 19th century it was known as Kleindeutschland—'Little Germany'. The sinking of the steamship *General Slocum* in 1904, carrying parishioners from St Mark's Church on an outing, killed 1,021 people and destroyed the German community. For most of the 20th century the neighbourhood lacked coherence. More immigrants arrived, including Hispanics (who dubbed it 'Loisaida'), Poles and Ukrainians. Squatters took over some buildings—this is the neighbourhood of the musical *Rent*—and St Mark's Place became the home of rebels.

1 | Exit the L subway at Third Avenue and walk one block east to Second Avenue. Turn right and walk south two blocks to the Village East Theater on 12th Street.

This stretch of Second Avenue, lined with Yiddish-language theatres, was known as the Jewish Rialto. Only a handful of original structures remain; the grandest is the Village East cinema (notice the cornerstone date in English and Hebrew). If possible, look inside the front doors at the Moorish carved ceiling. If you see a film here, do so in the main cinema upstairs, which has its elaborate décor completely preserved.

2 | Continue south on Second Avenue to reach 10th Street. Turn right and then enter the churchyard of St Mark's in the Bowery.

Probably built on what had been the site of Peter Stuyvesant's chapel, this simple stone church is the second-oldest in the city. The Dutch Governor is buried beneath the building and his grave marker can be seen in the east wall, along with an imposing bust of him. It's said that Peter Stuyvesant haunts the church—the distinctive sound of his wooden leg (he'd lost the right one in battle) can be heard clomping along the floorboards. Also buried here briefly was dry goods magnate A. T. Stewart, worth over $40 million when he died. His body was stolen in 1878 and ransomed for $200,000. However, the thieves overestimated his widow's

WHERE TO EAT

🍴 THE MADRAS CAFÉ,
79 Second Avenue
(between 4th and 5th Streets);
Tel: 212-254-8002.
Particularly good in an area known for Indian food.

🍴 B & H VEGETARIAN RESTAURANT,
127 Second Avenue
(between 7th and St Mark's Place);
Tel: 212-505-8065.
A kosher dairy reminder of Second Avenue's heyday.

🍴 VESELKA,
144 Second Avenue (at 9th Street);
Tel: 212-228-9682.
This diner is a good example of the area's strong Polish character.

sentimentality—she wouldn't pay until the price had dropped considerably. Some believe that Stewart haunts the churchyard, annoyed to this day at his wife's meanness.

3 | Two streets intersect in front of the church. Take Stuyvesant Street, which heads off at a diagonal, to 21 Stuyvesant Street.

This 1803 home was built by Petrus Stuyvesant, great-grandson of the Governor, as a wedding present for his daughter Elizabeth when she married tionary War soldier Nicholas Fish. Their

10

DISTANCE **2 miles (3.2km)**

ALLOW **1 hour**

START **Third Avenue station, L train**

FINISH **Second Avenue station, F/V train**

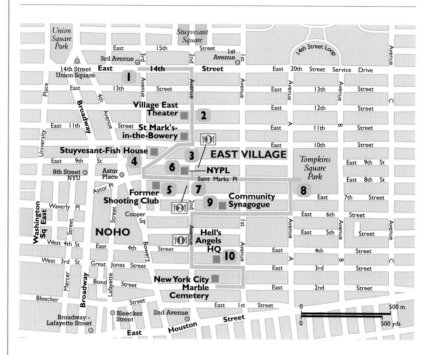

son Hamilton was born here and went on to a distinguished career in politics as a governor of New York, a senator and Ulysses S. Grant's secretary of state. This is the grandest old house preserved from this era. In 2001, the house was donated to Cooper Union, which now uses it as its President's house.

4 Continue west on Stuyvesant Street to Third Avenue. Turn left and walk one short block to St Mark's Place. Turn left again and walk to 12 St Mark's Place.

Built in 1885 for the German–American Shooting Society (note their name, in German, running across the façade), this building is one of the few historic landmarks on this street. It is also one of the last real traces of German influence remaining on a street that once boasted a plethora of private clubs, German beer halls and theatres.

5 Turn and look over on the opposite side of the street at numbers 19-25 St Mark's Place.

Once home to Arlington Hall, a German community centre and ballroom, and the Polish National Home (the 'Dom'), this was the site of Andy Warhol's Electric Circus, which featured the Velvet Underground as the house band. At his 'Exploding Plastic Inevitable', Warhol invited people to 'play games, dress as they like, dance, sit, think, tune in and turn on.' A recent renovation has altered the façade and invited in a series of chain restaurants and shops, causing long-time East Villagers to curse the suburbanization of the space; the addition of a gift shop for the now-defunct nightclub CBGBs didn't help the situation.

6 Walk east on St Mark's Place to Second Avenue. Turn left and walk to the Ottendorfer branch of the New York Public Library.

Oswald Ottendorfer, publisher of the influential German-language newspaper *Staats-Zeitung*, and wife Anna donated land here for a dispensary and free lending library in 1884. Both institutions managed to stay true to their missions for over a century. These Queen Anne-meets-Romanesque style buildings designed by William Schickel feature impressive terracotta decorations, in particular the scientists and doctors on the clinic—note the portrait busts of Galenus, Aesculapius, Hippocrates and Celsius surrounding the doorway.

OTTENDORFER BRANCH OF THE NEW YORK PUBLIC LIBRARY;
MON, WED, THU 10–6, TUE 1–8, FRI–SAT 1–5;
TEL: 212-674-0947

7 Return to St Mark's Place and walk east to Avenue A. This is the main street of the East Village and showcases the eclectic nature of the neighbourhood. Enter Tompkins Square Park on any path you choose.

Daniel Tompkins, a New York Governor and Vice President, lent his name and his property to what was one of the only open spaces in the 1811 street grid of Manhattan. Originally designated a produce market, the city acquired the land for parkland and, later, for a military parade ground. The area has long been linked to civil unrest; in 1874 a labour protest here grew into a bloody riot. Then in the 1980s police and residents clashed over enforcing the park's closing hours, which in effect barred the homeless from sleeping there. To solve the problem, the city closed the park in 1991 for a year in order to carry out renovation work. (The homeless residents were either evicted or relocated at this point, depending on whose side of the story you believe.) Of note in the park is the *General Slocum* memorial, a small fountain located in a playground towards the northern side. Surprisingly, this small marble stele of a boy and girl is the only commemoration of the steamship's sinking in June 1904—at 1,021 souls, the largest single loss of life in New York City's history prior to the World Trade Center attack. Also of interest is the Temperance Fountain, erected in 1888 and designed to convince local residents that municipal water was healthy and good to drink.

73

8 Leave Tompkins Square Park at its southwest corner, where Avenue A intersects 7th Street. Walk south one block on Avenue A to 6th Street. Turn right and walk to the Community Synagogue at 325 East 6th Street.

Originally, this building housed St Mark's Lutheran Church, the home parish of the victims of the *General Slocum* disaster. Historians estimate that every single block of Kleindeutschland lost at least one family. After 1904, Germans left the neighbourhood in droves, settling in Yorkville on the Upper East Side.

9 Continue on 6th Street to Second Avenue. Turn left and walk three blocks south to 3rd Street. Turn left and walk to the Hell's Angels clubhouse at 77 East 3rd Street.

When the motorcycle club Hell's Angels moved into this building in 1969, they were at the peak of their influence as counterculture rebels, epitomizing the lifestyle captured in Dennis Hopper's cult movie *Easy Rider*. Then came the Altamont Speedway concert—where a gun-toting fan was killed by Hell's Angels hired to work security—and accusations of violence and drug sales, which continue to plague the organization to this day. The government tried to seize this building in the 1990s as part of a drug investigation, but the charge was rebuffed in court. More recently, a woman was beaten nearly to death outside the building in early 2007, but the Hell's Angels claim no knowledge of her or the incident.

10 Continue east on 3rd Street to First Avenue. Turn right and walk one block south. Turn right on 2nd Street and walk half a block west to the New York City Marble Cemetery.

Manhattan has only two cemeteries still accepting in-ground burials; both are called 'Marble Cemetery' and both are located in this neighbourhood. In 1851, the city—fearing that it would run out of real estate—banned burials except for the paying tenants of these privately run graveyards. The most famous people buried here were President James Monroe, whose body was here from 1831 until 1858, when it was removed to Virginia, and the humorously named Preserved Fish, whose vault marker has been causing snickers since 1846.

For the nearest subway, continue on to Second Avenue, then turn left and walk south to Houston Street.

Secrets of Gramercy Park

This walk allows a tantalizing glimpse of one of New York's most exclusive neighbourhoods and attempts to unlock its hidden history.

Gramercy Park, a privately owned square, has always fascinated New Yorkers—especially those who can only stand outside the wrought-iron fence and look in. Modeled on London's Belgravia, the park became fashionable in the 1840s as wealthy New Yorkers began to move north from Greenwich Village. The neighbourhood has remarkably long-term residents: in a city known for the restless quest for the 'right' address, those who choose to live in Gramercy have a tendency to stay put. However, beneath the neighbourhood's staid exterior lie a host of intriguing stories, including a paranoiac's escape tunnel, a pair of fake houses, an actor dying in his garret on a dark and stormy night, and a public park in danger of returning to its donor if children are allowed to play in it. The National Arts Club (stop 4) has art galleries open to the public; it's worth calling ahead if you'd like to include them. If you want access to the park itself, find out when Gramercy Park Day (usually a Saturday in May) or the Christmas carols are taking place. These are the only days when the park is open to the public.

| Exit the R/W subway at the 23rd Street station and walk south on Broadway to 20th Street. Turn left and walk half a block to the Theodore Roosevelt birthplace at 28 East 20th Street.

Theodore Roosevelt, the only US President born and raised in New York City, lived in a house on this spot from his birth in 1858 until 1872. However, this is not that house. His boyhood home was razed to the ground in 1916, but when Roosevelt died in 1919, an organization was born within weeks to buy back the land and build a meticulous recreation of the house from Roosevelt's era. Filled with period furniture, the museum offers an interesting view into the Gilded Age.

THEODORE ROOSEVELT HOUSE;

TUE–SAT 9–5; TEL: 212-260-1616;
www.nps.gov/thrb

2 Continue to walk east on 20th Street, crossing Park Avenue South, and proceed to the corner of Gramercy Park South and Gramercy Park West on your left.

Gramercy is the English corruption of the Dutch *krom moersje* or 'crooked swamp', an apt description of the area in the colonial era, and not the Gramercy ('grant us mercy') found in Shakespeare. Developer Samuel Ruggles envisioned a private enclave where access to the park would bolster property values, but had trouble selling lots until the arrival of indoor plumbing in the early 1840s made land this far north of the old city desirable. Ruggles is responsible for the two broad avenues that terminate at the park: Lexington to the north (named after the first battle of the American Revolution) and Irving Place to the south, named after his friend, writer Washington Irving. These were the first avenues added to the Manhattan street grid after its publication in 1811. The park is owned cooperatively by the 60 surrounding lot owners and is governed by a board of five lifetime trustees. Access is by key only (both in and out) and the lock is changed annually to thwart key duplication. The statue in the centre of the park shows actor Edwin Booth—who lived at 16 Gramercy Park South—as Hamlet, his most famous role.

3 Walk to 4 Gramercy Park West.

11

DISTANCE 1 mile (1.6km)

ALLOW 45 minutes (more with museum and gallery visits)

START 23rd Street station, R/W trains

FINISH Third Avenue station, L train

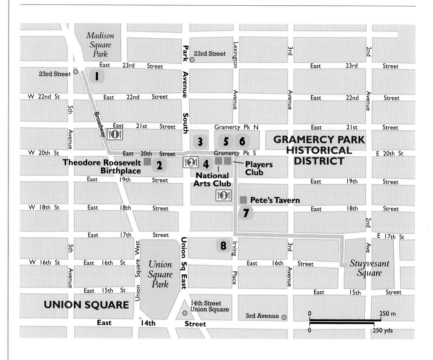

For many years, the only homes in New York with twin lamps marking their entrances were those of the current and former mayors. This house—the best preserved home from Gramercy Park's earliest development—belonged to Mayor James Harper, who is better known as the founder of Harper & Bros, publishers of the influential social and political magazine, *Harpers*.

4 Walk to 15 Gramercy Park South.

This double-wide townhouse was the home of New York's Governor, Samuel J. Tilden, who won the 1876 US Presidential election but—due to electoral shenanigans—never became president. Tilden retired to this home and hired Calvert Vaux, co-architect of Central Park, to 'Victorianize' the façade and oversee a complete interior renovation. Notable features include a gigantic stained-glass dome over what was once Tilden's library. Tilden grew paranoid in his later life (having had an

II

WHERE TO EAT

[O] **MAYROSE,**
920 Broadway (at 21st Street);
Tel: 212-533-3663.
Casual neighbourhood diner.

[O] **L'EXPRESS,**
249 Park Ave South (at 20th Street);
Tel: 212-254-5858.
French bistro; good food but
seemingly always busy.

[O] **FRIEND OF A FARMER,**
77 Irving Place (between 18th
and 19th Streets);
Tel: 212-477-2188.
Known for its use of local produce;
great brunch place.

election stolen from him) and there are persistent rumours of an escape tunnel he built from the house to 19th Street. Upon his death, Tilden left the bulk of his fortune to create the New York Public Library. The house fell into disrepair until rescued by the National Arts Club in 1906. Founded in 1896, the club promotes art and artists in all disciplines and was notable for accepting women as full members from its inception. In addition to members-only events, the club houses four small galleries which feature a rotating series of exhibits.

THE NATIONAL ARTS CLUB;
OPENING HOURS VARY; TEL: 212-475-3424

5 Look next door at 16 Gramercy Park South.

Edwin Booth was probably the best known tragedian of his age, but a portion of his fame was eclipsed in 1865 when his brother, John Wilkes Booth, assassinated Abraham Lincoln. Booth lived in this townhouse and in later life had it remodelled by architect Stanford White as the Players Club, a private membership organization designed to bring actors and their patrons together outside the theatre. Booth kept a small apartment for himself in the garret; one particularly tempestuous night, he expired in his bed, and it's said the newly installed electric street lights around the park instantly sputtered out. The Players keeps Booth's rooms as they were when he died, but public access is limited.

6 Continue east to Irving Place. Turn right and walk two blocks south to 18th Street where you will see Pete's Tavern on the northeast corner.

Pete's Tavern lays claim to being one of New York's oldest drinking establishments, though the date on the awning, 1864, is certainly not correct. In fact, the tavern is probably more than a decade older. It stayed in business during Prohibition by posing as a harmless flower shop—knowledgeable patrons walked through the refrigerated flower case into the bar beyond. Writer O. Henry was a regular here, and the booth where he allegedly wrote his most famous story, *The Gift of the Magi*, is preserved, though he is more likely to have written it in his nearby home after a night of drinking at Pete's.

7 Continue south on Irving Place one block to the corner of 17th Street.

The small house on the southwest corner of this intersection bears a beautiful plaque declaring it the former home of writer Washington Irving. Irving became popular after the publication of his satirical *History of New York*, which also launched the term 'Knickerbocker' to describe old New York families. By the time Samuel Ruggles named this street after Irving, the author had composed his most durable tales, including *The Legend of Sleepy Hollow* and *Rip Van Winkle*. However, Irving never lived in this home—or anywhere on this street for that matter. Ruggles simply wanted to commemorate the man he regarded as America's greatest living author; it is later generations who needed to forge a physical connection between Irving and the street. This small house seemed old enough to fit the mythology.

8 Head east on 17th Street two blocks to the corner of Rutherford Place. Turn right, walk one block to 16th Street and enter Stuyvesant Square.

All of the land surrounding this park was originally the farm of Dutch Governor Peter Stuyvesant. In 1836, his descendant, Peter Gerard Stuyvesant, gave this parcel to the city as a place of 'peace and quiet'. Already divided by Second Avenue, the park was developed as two symmetrical halves. The section to the west includes a 1941 statue of Governor Peter Stuyvesant by Gertrude Vanderbilt

Whitney, the sculptor better known as the founder of the Whitney Museum of Art. In the 1930s, Parks Commissioner Robert Moses attempted to install a playground in the park but was presented with a lawsuit filed by local hospitals; they complained of the potential noise disrupting their patients' convalescence. The playground was abandoned when the courts agreed children playing would indeed violate the bequest's 'peace and quiet' clause and that the land would therefore revert to the Stuyvesant family. For the nearest L train subway, walk south to 14th Street and west one block to Third Avenue; alternatively, walk west three blocks on 16th Street to reach the Union Square Station of the N/R/Q/W, 6 and L trains.

Chelsea Transformations

Discover a neighbourhood where academics rub shoulders with clubbers and 19th-century factories have been reborn as 21st-century art galleries.

Today's Chelsea occupies much of Major Thomas Clarke's farm, and was named by him, presumably after the London borough of Chelsea. His grandson, Clement Clarke Moore, inherited the property in 1816. A noted Biblical scholar, Moore is today best known as the author of the poem *A Visit from St Nicholas* ('Twas the Night Before Christmas'), although this has recently been disputed. No trace of the farm exists. New York's expansion in the 1830s led to the eastern section being developed by Moore as residential lots, while the western section—close to piers and rails—became a warehouse district. After a period of decline in the 20th century, as cargo trains gave way to long-distance lorries, many warehouses transformed into contemporary art galleries. There are nearly 250 of them and they are the neighbourhood's most popular attraction. Plans are underway to convert the elevated cargo rail bed—the High Line—into a public park with access to new condos and museums. This is a lively area, especially on sunny Saturdays, with a young, hip and gay population.

1 Exit the A/C/E subway at 14th Street or the L at Eighth Avenue. You immediately see two former banks—the former New York Savings Bank building (now Balducci's) and the former New York County National Bank (now apartments and a spa).

Fourteenth Street serves as the southern border of Chelsea and a major commercial thoroughfare. These neo-classical banks are unusual in this neighbourhood of warehouses and factories for their oversized grandeur. The 1897 Balducci's building is by R.H. Robertson, who was simultaneously starting work on the Park Row building on City Hall Park, the world's tallest skyscraper. It is worth entering to see the interior architecture—in particular the massive dome—as well as the beautifully displayed gourmet food items.

2 Proceed one block west on 14th Street to Ninth Avenue. Turn right and walk one block to Chelsea Market.

This is the original factory of the North American Biscuit Company, Nabisco, where the mass-produced cookie in America was born. Built between 1902 and 1913 (and renovated in the 1990s), it now houses bakeries, speciality food stores and take-away and sit-down restaurants. It's worth entering even for non-shoppers to view the creative reuse of old industrial components: old pipe topped with glass serves as a table; rusted street lights line the exit hallway; the flour mill's water source is now a decorative fountain. (Upstairs are a number of private television studios.)

CHELSEA MARKET;

OPEN DAILY, EACH TENANT KEEPS SEPARATE HOURS; www.chelseamarket.com

DISTANCE **2.5 miles (4km)**

ALLOW **1.75 hours (longer with gallery visits)**

START **14th Street station, A/C/E trains (also known as the Eighth Avenue
station on the L train)**

FINISH **23rd Street station, 1 train**

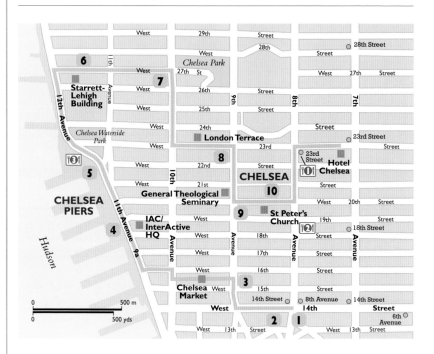

3 Walk through the Chelsea Market,
exiting on Tenth Avenue near 16th
Street. Notice as you cross Tenth Avenue
the High Line elevated railroad. This
allowed freight to travel the west side of
the island—through the buildings—
without impeding traffic. Walk west on
16th Street to Eleventh Avenue. Turn
right on Eleventh Avenue and go two
blocks to reach the IAC/InterActive
headquarters on 18th Street.

Although Frank Gehry is one of
America's leading architects, this is his
first building in New York, completed
in 2007 for IAC, a leading US Internet
company. Each of the nearly 1,500
frosted glass panels is specially crafted
and uniquely shaped. Other high-tech
companies are finding homes in Chelsea,
too; in 2006, Google moved to the
former Port Authority building across
Ninth Avenue from Chelsea Market.

4 Across Eleventh Avenue is Chelsea Piers. Walk four blocks northwards to reach 22nd Street, where Twelfth Avenue begins.

If you want to golf, ice skate, rock climb, eat or just get a closer look at the Hudson River, cross Eleventh Avenue to Chelsea Piers. Nine piers were built here early in the 20th century, including the berth where the *Titanic* was expected to arrive, but where instead, relatives gathered for news and for the *Carpathia* bringing the survivors. The piers now provide 30 acres of fun; even the neighbourhood canines come for exercise in the dog park section of Chelsea Waterside Park. Manhattan's largest film and TV production facility is also here, but is closed to the public.

CHELSEA PIERS;

TEL: 212-336-6666; www.chelseapiers.com

5 Proceed north on Twelfth Avenue (or on the pedestrian/bike path in Hudson River Park) to the Starrett-Lehigh Building between 26th and 27th Streets. Turn right onto 27th Street and walk on the north side to view this massive building.

Built in 1932 by Cory & Cory, (with Yasuo Matsui) the Starrett-Lehigh Building sits on top of a former freight terminal and has elevators inside—still in use—that can carry entire rail cars. Now the home of upscale tenants like Martha Stewart and Hugo Boss, the architecture greatly influenced Frank Lloyd Wright and Philip Johnson. (It was one of the few American buildings Johnson presented in MoMA's influential 1932 exhibition that coined the term 'International Style'.) Note

WHERE TO EAT

|O| **MURRAY'S BAGELS,**
242 Eighth Avenue (between 22nd and 23rd Streets).
Tel: 646-638-1335.
Some extensive but quick bagel and deli options.

|O| **ROOM SERVICE,**
166 Eighth Avenue (between 18th and 19th Streets);
Tel: 212-691-0299.
Contemporary Thai cuisine and fun drinks in a whimsical space.

|O| **RUTHY'S BAKERY & CAFÉ,**
in Chelsea Piers (at 23rd Street);
Tel: 212-336-6333.
Casual dining by the waterfront.

the undulating setbacks on the upper floors as well as the small-paned glass windows—over 8 miles (12.87km) of glass in all—that seem to open in completely random configurations.

6 Continue east on 27th Street, crossing Eleventh Avenue.

This is the city's most densely packed block of trendy nightclubs. During the day, the only activity here centres on a few galleries and car repair/salvage operations. But if you were to return after midnight, you would see scores of young people queuing in front of old warehouses with vaguely discernable signs that separate each club's frontage.

(If you're fashionable enough to get in, you know in advance which velvet rope and bouncer you're aiming for.)

7 Turn right on Tenth Avenue and walk south to 23rd Street. The blocks to your right between Tenth and Eleventh Avenues are dense with galleries (closed Sun and Mon) and may demand a detour. Notable galleries include: White Box (26th Street); Cheim & Read (25th Street); Matthew Marks, Mary Boone, Gagosian, Barbara Gladstone (24th Street); Jim Kempner Fine Arts (23rd Street). After 'gallery hopping', turn left onto 23rd Street and walk east towards Ninth Avenue, stopping at London Terrace.

The name of this complex comes not from its architecture, but from the previous row of houses built here. Although when the 1,670-apartment complex first opened, the doormen *did* dress as London Bobbies. On the south side of 23rd Street, a fine row of Anglo-Italianate homes serves as a reminder of what fashionable Chelsea looked like in the 1850s.

FOR DETAILS OF GALLERIES:
www.chelseaartgalleries.com

8 Turn right on Ninth Avenue and head south to the General Theological Seminary, which takes up the block between 20th and 21st Streets.

From Monday to Saturday, visitors with ID can obtain a pass in the lobby to visit the seminary gardens. Alternately, detour west on 20th Street between Ninth and Tenth Avenues for a peek into the close. The school was founded in 1817 as the first Episcopal seminary in America and moved to Chelsea when Clement Clarke Moore (who also taught at the school) offered them 66 lots. Inside the close, the buildings harmoniously blend a number of different eras, but the bell tower of the seminary chapel (about 1888 by Charles Haight) dominates.

GENERAL THEOLOGICAL SEMINARY;
MON–FRI 12–3, SAT 11–3; TEL: 212-243-5150

9 Cross Ninth Avenue at 20th Street and head east to 346 West 20th Street.

The boxy Greek Revival building, next to St Peter's Church, is now the rectory, but was the church's original 1832 home, built on land donated by Clement Clarke Moore. By the time St Peter's main building was completed six years later, the parish had embraced the Gothic Revival style, making this the first such church in New York. The former church hall, just east of the church, is now home to the Atlantic Theater Company, David Mamet and William H. Macy's revered off-Broadway troupe.

10 Continue east on 20th Street to Eighth Avenue, turn left and walk three blocks north to 23rd Street. Turn right on 23rd Street and walk almost a full block to the Hotel Chelsea.

The Hotel Chelsea began life as a (failed) cooperative apartment house in 1883

and was reborn as a hotel in 1905. One of the city's most famed literary landmarks, it has been the home of novelists (Arthur Clark, Thomas Wolfe), playwrights (Arthur Miller), musicians ("staying up for days in the Chelsea Hotel, writing 'Sad Eyed Lady of the Lowlands' for You," sang Bob Dylan) and visual artists (Andy Warhol's entourage). The hotel has also seen its share of tragic endings. Resident Welsh poet Dylan Thomas died here after downing a record number of whiskies at the White Horse Tavern and Sid Vicious' girlfriend, Nancy, was stabbed to death (by Vicious?) in Room 100. For the nearest subway, continue to the corner of Seventh Avenue for the 1 train.

From Flatiron to Empire State

Framed by two of the city's most important skyscrapers, this area offers Beaux Arts grandeur as well as modern steel and glass.

In 1811, the city published the Commissioners' Plan, which laid out the rigid street grid of Manhattan, set uniform house lots and got rid of older roads. During development, however, the main road—Broadway—was considered too important to remove. Because it runs diagonally, it cuts across the avenues creating small, triangular plots of land. New Yorkers dubbed these 'squares' and the first one to develop was Madison Square. (Technically, Madison Square is the median between Fifth Avenue and Broadway, not the nearby park.) On the grid, this area was designated a military parade ground, but when that never materialized, the space was altered into the present Madison Square Park, landscaped by Ignaz Pilat, chief gardener of Central Park. The area covered on this tour often defies characterization, in part because it encompasses everything from high-rise office towers to elegant old mansions. However, this is part of its charm, as you'll be able to see a wide variety of New York buildings in a small area. The Church of the Incarnation is a highlight, so you may wish to plan your tour for a time that it will be open to visitors.

| Exit the R/W subway at 23rd Street and cross into Madison Square Park. Stop at the statue of William Seward at the park's southwest corner.

The former New York Governor, William Seward, was a leading Republican presidential candidate in 1860. A compromise gave the nod to Abraham Lincoln and Seward became the Secretary of State. He is most famous for purchasing Alaska from the Russians in 1867. After Seward died, money was raised for this memorial; when funds ran short, artist Randolph Rogers took pieces of a Lincoln sculpture he'd created, slightly rearranged them, and grafted Seward's head on to it, turning the statesman into the lanky, Lincolnesque man you see here.

2 Turn from the statue to look across 23rd Street at the Flatiron Building.

Officially the Fuller Building, this is the most famous early skyscraper in New York—so famous, in fact, that it's often called the first skyscraper in the city (it wasn't) and the world's tallest (it wasn't that, either). Opened in 1902, it is the only New York skyscraper by Daniel Burnham (of Burnham & Root), the leader of the 'Chicago School' that perfected steel-frame construction. Its nickname derives from the shape of its lot, a triangle reminiscent of a flat iron. But what the building resembles most is a steamship sailing up Fifth Avenue. The undulating façade suggests waves lapping against its hull. No surface is free of

ornamentation—even the plain stones are rough hewn—making this the last fully decorated skyscraper and still one of the most beautiful ever constructed.

3 Walk deeper into Madison Square Park to find a good view of the Metropolitan Life tower on Madison Avenue between 23rd and 24th Streets.

Pierre LeBrun modelled the soaring tower of Metropolitan Life—the world's tallest in 1909—on the campanile in Piazza San Marco in Venice. Its most notable feature was its giant four-faced clock. However, within a few years, the building had been eclipsed and by the time the Empire State Building was being built, Met Life was no longer even a mid-sized skyscraper. In 1930, the company broke ground next door on a 100-storey

DISTANCE 1 mile (1.6km)

ALLOW 1 hour

START 23rd Street station, R/W trains

FINISH 34th Street station, N/Q/R/W and B/D/F/V trains

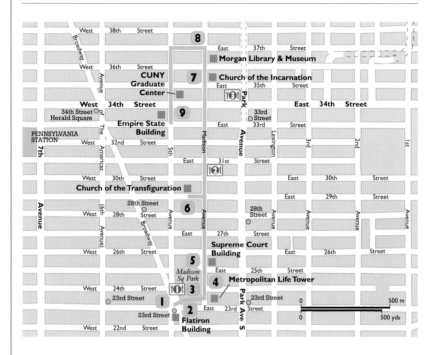

tower designed by Harvey Wiley Corbett to restore the company's prominence. The 29-storey base between 24th and 25th Streets is all that was finished before the Depression halted further construction. It was capped off as the Met Life annexe.

4 Walk to the Supreme Court Building at the corner of Madison Avenue and 25th Street.

Of all the Beaux Arts courthouses in New York, this Supreme Court building by James Brown Lord is the most richly detailed—a full third of the budget was reserved purely for decoration. Marble statues depicting Wisdom and Force flank the entrance and the cornice is lined with the great philosophers and law givers, including Moses and Confucius. Though not immediately noticeable, a statue to the far right of the main entrance is missing. Here stood Mohammed; he was removed in the 1950s out of respect for the Muslim prohibition regarding depictions of the Prophet.

5 Walk four blocks north on Madison Avenue to 29th Street, then turn left and proceed to the Church of the Transfiguration.

When actor Joseph Jefferson approached a nearby church to hold the funeral of his fellow thespian George Holland, the church refused (actors, evidently, being too dissolute for proper burial) and referred him to that 'little church around the corner'. The name stuck and this has long been considered the theatrical church. Among those married here were P.G. Wodehouse and Sam Waterston. It was also used as a setting in the television show *Sex and the City*. Inside, note the stained-glass windows of actors, including Jefferson, Holland and Edwin Booth.

6 Retrace your steps to Madison Avenue. Turn left and walk six blocks north to 35th Street and the Church of the Incarnation.

The Church of the Incarnation began as a mission parish of Grace Church in Greenwich Village, for those who couldn't afford Grace's exorbitant pew rent. This Decorated Gothic structure by E. T. Littell opened in 1864. A terrible fire in 1882 left most of the church in ashes; it was rebuilt and expanded over the next 30 years. The sumptuous interior features the work of artists of the late 19th century, including John LaFarge, Louis Comfort Tiffany, Daniel Chester French, Edward Burne-Jones and William Morris.

CHURCH OF THE INCARNATION;

MON–WED, FRI, 11.30–2; TEL: 212-689-6350

7 Walk one block north to the Morgan Library & Museum, between 36th and 37th Streets.

'Mr Morgan's Library' opened in 1906 as a repository for the financier's growing collection of illuminated manuscripts, books and old master paintings. Designed by Charles McKim in the style of a Renaissance palazzo, it has a stunning interior and is one of McKim's finest works. A decade after his father's death, J.P. 'Jack' Morgan, Jr, opened the library as a public museum. An annexe was built next door and, in 1988, Jack Morgan's home was also added to the complex. In 2006, the disparate elements were given a unifying modern shell by Renzo Piano that also expanded the museum's exhibition space by over 50 percent.

MORGAN LIBRARY & MUSEUM;

TUE–SUN; TEL: 212-685-0008;

www.morganlibrary.org

WHERE TO EAT

🍴 SHAKE SHACK,
in Madison Square Park;
Tel: 212-889-6600.
Gourmet burgers and fries; hands
down the most popular lunch spot
in the area.

🍴 SUBTLE TEA,
121 Madison Avenue (at 30th Street);
Tel: 212-481-4713.
Wide selection of teas, coffees
and sandwiches.

🍴 FRANCHIA,
12 Park Avenue (between
34th and 35th Streets);
Tel: 212-213-1001.
Elegant Korean tea parlour.

8 Turn west onto 37th Street and
walk to Fifth Avenue. Turn left on
Fifth Avenue and walk south two blocks
to the former B. Altman Building (now
the Graduate Center of CUNY), which
is between 35th and 34th Streets.

When it opened in 1906, B. Altman &
Company was the first grand shopping
emporium on Fifth Avenue. Designed
by Trowbridge & Livingston (who also
built Morgan's Bank on Wall Street), the
store, although massive, was designed to
harmonize with the residential character
of the neighbourhood. Throughout its
life, the store generated its own power
and, during the famous New York
blackout of 1965, its lights blazed through

the night as people came to seek shelter.
The store closed in 1989; in the 1990s,
it was renovated to house the CUNY
Graduate Center and part of the New
York Public Library.

9 Turn to look at the huge edifice of
the Empire State Building.

Not just the tallest building in the world
when it opened in 1931, but the most
massive office tower ever conceived—it
had rentable floor space over twice the
size of the rival Chrysler Building. In
order that it not be accused of hoisting
a useless spire (a charge levelled at
the Chrysler Building), the architects
announced the Empire State's spire would
serve as a mooring mast for an airship.
This was folly—aeronautical engineers
fully understood that tying a zeppelin
to the skyscraper would be impossible.
However, this didn't stop the building's
publicity agents from attempting an
airship delivery of newspapers for the
newsreel cameras. After it opened, it was
soon dubbed the 'Empty State'. While
the Depression had allowed architects
Shreve, Lamb & Harmon to come in
under budget, it also meant there weren't
enough viable tenants. For years the
only lucrative part of the building was
its 86th-floor observatory, still one of
the great destinations in New York. The
102nd floor is now also open to visitors.
EMPIRE STATE BUILDING;
DAILY 8AM–2AM; www.esbnyc.com
Turn right onto 34th Street and continue
to Sixth Avenue for the N/R/W/Q and
B/D/F/V 34th Street station.

Across 42nd Street

From the 'Crossroads of the World' to the expansive UN Headquarters, this walk allows you to survey the street that really defines New York.

For most of the 19th century, 42nd Street was at best an inconvenient destination. Commodore Vanderbilt's railways deposited passengers at the Grand Central Depot and vast stables and carriage shops lined Longacre Square. However, at the dawn of the 20th century, everything changed. The old depot was torn down for a new Grand Central Terminal, the imposing public library—perhaps New York's most impressive building—was under construction on Fifth Avenue, and Longacre Square was redubbed Times Square in honour of its successful new tenant, the New York Times. Making all of this possible was New York's most ambitious project of the era—the IRT subway, which connected residential Upper West Side neighbourhoods to the Financial District via an east-west crossover along 42nd Street. Before the advent of the subway, 42nd Street was just another thoroughfare; after the subway's opening, it was the nexus of a brand-new 'Midtown' district that would soon have a musical named after it and become synonymous with the glitz and glamour of New York City itself.

I Exit the subway at Times Square station and walk west on 42nd Street to the staircase of the New Victory Theater at 330 West 42nd Street.

To many, the name 42nd Street evokes the 'beat of dancing feet' conjured up by the lyrics of the musical *42nd Street*. Indeed, although we call them 'Broadway' theatres, 42nd Street was the neighbourhood's first real entertainment avenue, with venues such as the Republic (now the New Victory) opening in 1900 and, across the street, the New Amsterdam, which opened in 1903. By 1925, nearly a dozen theatres lined this one block of 42nd Street. After World War II, most were converted to burlesque houses or cinemas, which soon degraded to showing mostly pornography. It was a concerted effort in the late 1980s and early 1990s that cleaned up the street, beginning with Walt Disney's thorough makeover of the old New Amsterdam theatre. Next door, where McDonald's now graces the marquee, is the Candler Building, a 1915 skyscraper named after Asa Candler, the man who made Coca Cola a household name, but whose own name is largely forgotten.

2 Head east on 42nd Street to Times Square. Turn left and walk up to 44th Street. Cross over to the middle of the square and look south at the skyscraper at the southern end of the square—the former *New York Times* headquarters—distinguished by the famous news 'zipper'.

WHERE TO EAT

[IOI] JUNIOR'S,
1515 Broadway (at 45th Street);
Tel: 212-302-2000.
The best New York cheesecake.

[IOI] JOHN'S PIZZERIA TIMES SQUARE, 260 West 44th (between Broadway and Eighth Avenue);
Tel: 212-391-7560.
Hand-made pizza served in a glorious old church.

[IOI] THE CAMPBELL APARTMENT,
Inside Grand Central Terminal;
Tel: 212-953-0409.
Formerly a private office and now one of the best bars in the city; respectable clothing required.

As financier August Belmont was building the city's first subway, he convinced the *New York Times* to move its operations to 42nd Street and build a skyscraper with a subway station in its basement. At the same time, Belmont prodded city officials to rename Longacre Square in honour of its illustrious new tenant. The *Times* rang in the New Year in 1905 with a rooftop fireworks display from this tower; a few years later, dangerous fireworks were replaced by the famous ball. (Even when the ball is not in place, you can still see its pole jutting up from the roofline.) The ball represents a 'dropping ball' which was an antiquated form of daily timekeeping—in the early days of telegraphy, a ball was dropped

OPPOSITE: TIMES SQUARE

DISTANCE 1.5 miles (2.45km)

ALLOW 1.5 hours

START Times Square station, 1/2/3, N/Q/R/S/W and 7 trains

FINISH Grand Central Terminal

from the Western Union office at noon, allowing those with pocket watches to keep more accurate time. Advertisements are now required by law on every building in Times Square (to preserve the look of the neighbourhood). The billboards on the old Times Tower are costly to rent—however, with New Year's Eve celebrations broadcast to over one billion people, these advertisements are probably the most visible you can get.

3 Return to 42nd Street and walk one block east to the corner of Sixth Avenue and Bryant Park.

Bryant Park is named after the poet and journalist William Cullen Bryant, a driving force behind the creation of Central Park. A rather severe statue of Bryant sits near the Bryant Park Café, glowering out at visitors. The park hosted New York's Crystal Palace Exposition which, like its London counterpart, served to show off American engineering. Most famously, Elisha Otis demonstrated his elevator safety brake here in 1854. Today, the park hosts a wide variety of events, including free summer movies, Fashion Week's couture shows, a holiday market in December and a skating rink.

4 Leave Bryant Park on 42nd Street, heading towards Fifth Avenue. Circle around the front of the New York Public Library on Fifth Avenue between 40th and 42nd Streets.

This main research branch of the New York Public Library is a marvel inside and out. Built by Carèrre & Hastings and opened in 1911, this is, along with Grand Central, the zenith of Beaux Arts architecture in New York. The lions that flank the entrance were nicknamed Patience and Fortitude by Mayor Fiorello LaGuardia during the depression. Atop the cornice, figures representing arts and letters flank the names of the men whose separate collections gave birth to the library in 1886: John Jacob Astor, James Lenox and former New York Governor Samuel J. Tilden. It is worth climbing to the top floor to admire the building's crowning glory—the two-block-long main reading room that is probably the most important research space in America. The millions of books and other items that make up the collection are kept in acres of storage on the lower floors, including vaults underneath Bryant Park.

NEW YORK PUBLIC LIBRARY;
TUE–SUN; TEL: 212-930-0830; www.nypl.org

5 Return to 42nd Street and walk east to Vanderbilt Avenue and Grand Central Terminal.

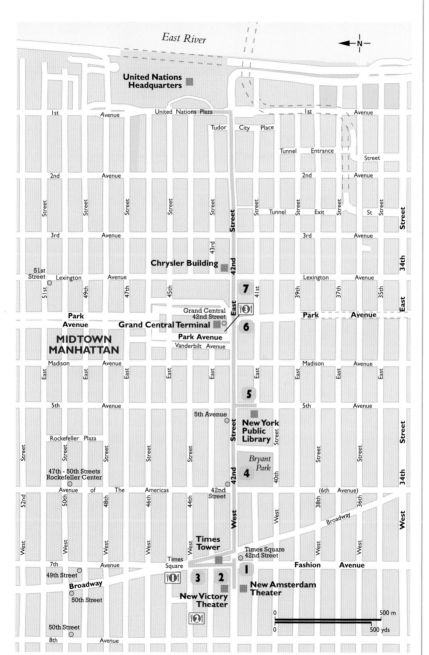

East River

N

United Nations
Headquarters

United Nations Plaza

Tudor City Place

Tunnel Entrance

Street

2nd Avenue

2nd Avenue

Tunnel Exit

St Street

3rd Avenue

3rd Avenue

34th

43rd

42nd

Chrysler Building

51st
Street

Lexington Avenue

Lexington Avenue

39th

37th

35th

41st

7

East

Park
Avenue

Grand Central
42nd Street

Grand Central Terminal

Park Avenue

6

Park Avenue

MIDTOWN
MANHATTAN

Vanderbilt Avenue

Madison Avenue

Madison Avenue

5

5th Avenue

5th Avenue

5th Avenue

New York
Public
Library

Rockefeller Plaza

Bryant
Park

40th

47th – 50th Streets
Rockefeller Center

42nd
Street

4

Avenue of The Americas

(6th Avenue)

52nd

50th

48th

46th

44th

Broadway

36th

West

42nd
Street

West

West

Times
Tower

Times
Square

Times Square
42nd Street

Fashion Avenue

7th Avenue

49th Street

Broadway

3

2

1

New Amsterdam
Theater

50th Street

New Victory
Theater

50th Street

0   500 m

8th Avenue

0   500 yds

Cornelius Vanderbilt began his career in steamships, earning the nickname 'The Commodore', but by 1871 had gained a controlling interest in two of New York's largest railroad companies and built a Grand Central Depot at 42nd Street. The electrification of the train system at the turn of the 20th century spurred Vanderbilt's son, William, to commission this even grander Grand Central, by the firm Warren & Wetmore, which opened in 1913. It is the largest railway terminal in the world. The statues on top of the Tiffany clock on the building's 42nd Street entrance depict Mercury, god of commerce, supported by Hera (wisdom) and Hercules (strength). Below the clock, a figure of the Commodore in his wool coat greets passing motorists. Inside, the main hall has been meticulously restored; a century's worth of grime came off the beautiful star-laden ceiling. Follow the zodiac diagonally across the ceiling to the northwest corner—there, you'll see a black 1 by 2ft (0.30 by 0.61m) rectangle, one small patch left in its filthy state to show the remarkable contrast.

6 Leave Grand Central and cross back to the south side of 42nd Street for views of the Chrysler Building on the corner of Lexington Avenue.

In 1929, this skyscraper and the Manhattan Company on Wall Street were in stiff competition to be the tallest in the world. All signs pointed to the Manhattan Company's victory until Chrysler's architect, William Van Allen, revealed his secret weapon: a 125ft (38.1m)

spire he'd had constructed in the dome and winched out one afternoon. Long considered the pinnacle of Art Deco skyscraper design, the building's appeal comes in part from its visual complexity. The tall central shaft is sheathed in geometric white brick, punctuated by steel designs at the setbacks, winged braziers at one level (the 1928 Chrysler hood ornament), gigantic eagles at another. The dome is stainless Nirosta steel. This was the world's tallest building for only a year before being outdone by the Empire State Building, a skyscraper so large that the offices of two Chrysler Buildings would fit inside.

7 Continue east on 42nd Street to First Avenue. Turn left and walk to 44th Street to stand opposite the entrance to the United Nations.

After the founding of the United Nations in 1945, the United States formally requested that its home be based in the US. John D. Rockefeller, Jr, donated more than $8 million for the acquisition of this parcel of land fronting the East River in an area know as Turtle Bay. The main buildings—the low-slung General Assembly and the taller, glass Secretariat—are not officially credited to any one architect, but were built by Wallace K. Harrison (an architect of Rockefeller Center) based on an overall plan by Le Corbusier. There are currently 192 member nations and three non-member (observer) states. For the nearest subway, return to 42nd Street, turn right and continue to Grand Central Terminal.

HARLEM LINE DEPARTURES

MTA METRO-NORTH TICKETS

Modern Midtown

New York is defined by its skyline. This walk focuses on America's largest business district and the skyscrapers that changed modern architecture.

The speed of life in Midtown Manhattan sometimes makes it hard to appreciate its architecture, but some of the city's most important skyscrapers are found in this small area. Indeed, the Seagram Building (1958) and its neighbour Lever House (1952) are the two most important post-World War II skyscrapers in New York City and, perhaps, the world. They are responsible, for good or ill, for every glass curtain-wall structure since. And while Midtown didn't take off as a business district until after World War II, some of its most compelling skyscrapers are those built during the era of Art Deco experimentation, including Rockefeller Center, the world's greatest skyscraper complex. Seeing this neighbourhood amid the hustle and bustle of a weekday afternoon shows the skyscrapers as they were intended to be seen (sort of 'machines for working', to paraphrase Le Corbusier). But if you'd like a little more time for contemplation, go on a Sunday morning when you'll have this area virtually to yourself.

Exit the 6 subway at 51st Street. The former RCA Building (now General Electric) is on the southwest corner. Make sure you stand on the east side of Lexington Avenue to see the building from a good vantage.

This building, built for radio giant RCA, is a riot of Deco motifs including actual radio giants that stare down sternly from the parapets. Cross & Cross, like many architects of the period, use lightning bolts to convey the energy of radio waves; some are shooting out of clenched fists, a symbol of strength. RCA moved to Rockefeller Center to be replaced by General Electric, for whom the lightning-bolt motifs were equally appropriate. Also notice the brick facing matches that of St Bartholomew's church on Park Avenue, helping the building to fit into the context of the streetscape.

2 Proceed one block west on 51st Street to Park Avenue, turn right and walk north one block to the Seagram Building at 375 Park Avenue on your right.

Lead architect Mies van der Rohe was chosen for the Seagram Building because he straddled the line between the too-American Frank Lloyd Wright and the too-European Le Corbusier. This building is such a success because of its meticulous attention to detail: dark bronze window mullions; a lobby that seamlessly blends interior space with the adjoining plaza; and a sheer façade of amber glass made possible by hiding all the buildings 'guts'

away from the street. Much of the design details are by Philip Johnson, America's premier practitioner of the International Style. The wide plaza was controversial at the time, as the city was afraid fewer offices would lower tax revenues. However, new zoning regulations in the 1960s made such plazas standard. But where later plazas encourage people to linger, this one is designed for looks only—Mies even ordered that the water in the fountains always be kept as high as possible to make sure no one sat down.

3 Turn to look at Lever House across Park Avenue at 53rd Street.

Designed by Gordon Bunshaft of Skidmore, Owings & Merrill, this building's gleaming green glass façade was picked so that its owner, America's premier soap manufacturer, could demonstrate the efficiency of its products.

107

DISTANCE 1.3 miles (2.1km)

ALLOW 1 hour 15 minutes

START 51st Street station, 6 train

FINISH Fifth Avenue station, N/R/W trains

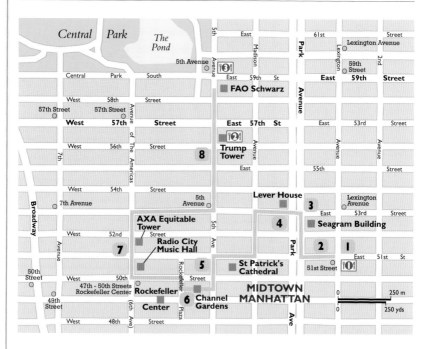

(To keep the glass façade looking its best, employees weren't allowed to have personal effects visible from the street; Seagram solved this problem by eliminating window sills.) The building is the first to feature complete climate control, so that there was no need for windows to ever open. Thus, the all-glass skyscraper was born. Every building built since bears some debt to this one. The second-storey garden overhangs the courtyard and originally included shuffleboard for lunchtime recreation.

4 Walk west on 53rd Street one block to Madison Avenue. Turn left and walk two blocks south. Turn right onto 51st Street to walk along the northern side of St Patrick's Cathedral, the entrance of which is on Fifth Avenue.

One way to comprehend the rapid changes in Midtown during the 20th century is simply to look at St Patrick's and be reminded that the site was picked in the 1850s for its rural character. Completed in 1878, this is architect

James Renwick's crowning glory, a soaring space in the best Gothic tradition. However, the nave is always humming with activity, which robs the space of some of its sanctity. Of note is the Lady Chapel, a later addition by Charles T. Mathews, and the grand front doors, which include a depiction of Elizabeth Ann Seton—a native New Yorker and the first American-born saint.

ST PATRICK'S CATHEDRAL;
DAILY 6.30AM–6.45PM; TEL: 212-753-2261

5 Walk one block south on Fifth Avenue and midway between 50th and 49th Streets you will find the 'Channel Gardens', the path into Rockefeller Center.

Rockefeller Center began as a way to build a new home for the Metropolitan Opera. John D. Rockefeller, Jr, negotiated a long-term land lease from Columbia University, but by the time the Center was ready for construction in 1931, the opera had backed out and RCA—owners of NBC radio—moved in. (They still have their headquarters in 30 Rockefeller Center, the tallest of the skyscrapers.) Additionally, Rockefeller had ambitious plans for the Center to be an economic League of Nations. Thus, flanking the Channel Gardens are the British Empire Building (north) and La Maison Française (south). Mussolini agreed to tenant an Italian building, but Hitler's German building never got off the ground. The subterranean level below the plaza held shops and restaurants. This type of indoor shopping arcade was a novelty in the 1930s, and was failing until the sunken plaza was converted into a skating rink. In winter, this is still the Center's biggest draw. Paul Manship's gold statue above the rink shows Prometheus stealing fire from the gods.

ROCKEFELLER CENTER;
OPEN 24 HOURS A DAY; TEL: 212-632-3975

WHERE TO EAT

🍴 **CAFÉ METRO,**
569 Lexington Ave (at 51st Street);
Tel: 212-697-7200.
Busy midtown lunch spot, with
everything from coffee to a pasta bar.

🍴 **TRUMP'S ICE CREAM PARLOR,**
Trump Tower (725 Fifth Avenue);
Tel: 212-836-3200.
Delightfully gleaming Americana.

🍴 **BOTTEGA DEL VINO,**
7 E 59th Street (at Fifth Avenue);
Tel: 212-223-3028.
Italian specialities with outdoor tables
in good weather.

6 Circle the plaza to 50th Street, walk
one block west to Sixth Avenue and
Radio City Music Hall is on your right.

The largest theatre in the city, the 6,000-
seat Radio City Music Hall opened in
1932. The roundels on the building's
50th Street side are by Hildreth Maier
and depict music, drama and dance. The
interiors were designed by Edward Durell
Stone and are sumptuous; seeing the
bathrooms alone is worth the price of a
ticket. By far the best-known show is the
annual Christmas Spectacular, which runs
for two months with as many as six shows
a day. Before you leave, look across Sixth
Avenue at the 'XYZ' buildings. These are
the post-war addition to the Rockefeller
Center holdings, built simultaneously
using virtually interchangeable plans.

7 Head north on Sixth Avenue (New
Yorkers never call it 'Avenue of the
Americas', its official name). If you have
time, stop in the AXA Equitable Tower
at No. 1290 to look at Thomas Hart
Benton's mural *America Today*. At 53rd
Street, turn right and walk one block
east to Fifth Avenue. Turn left and go
three blocks north to the southwest
corner of Fifth Avenue and 56th Street,
diagonally opposite from Trump Tower.

From this corner, you not only get a
good view of Der Scutt's Trump Tower,
with its surprising tree-laden setbacks,
but also Philip Johnson's AT&T building
on Madison Avenue (which has the
crown of the Chippendale armoire) and
Hugh Stubbins' Citicorp Center with its
asymmetrical top. Trump Tower, rather
than increase its height through tower-
in-a-plaza zoning, takes advantage of
changes to city regulations and provides
access in an enclosed atrium. The
highlight inside is the waterfall as well as
the sheer 'Trumpiness' of everything else.

8 Proceed two blocks up Fifth Avenue
to the General Motors Building at
767 Fifth Avenue.

Edward Durell Stone completed this
building in 1968 for GM. Its ground
floor now houses a CBS television studio,
toy giant FAO Schwarz and the Apple
Store. This is one of the places where the
open plaza is used to great effect, with
people lingering on a sunny day. The
nearest N/R/W subway station is at the
corner of 60th Street and Fifth Avenue.

The Silk Stocking District

Discover the contrasts on the Upper East Side, from marble mansions to wooden country estates, from elite Fifth Avenue to immigrant Yorkville.

The walk covers a wide expanse of the Upper East Side, traversing multiple neighbourhoods that range from top end to middle class. The walk begins in the area around Fifth Avenue and 59th Street (the so-called 'Gold Coast') where some of the city's most expensive apartments are located. The route passes elegant mansions and the grand Seventh Regiment Armory, whose wealthy volunteers could afford silk stockings and thus gave the nickname to this district. Beyond Park Avenue—where the New York Central Railroad still comes into the city underneath the street—you cross to the 'wrong side of the tracks', through the remnants of Czech, Hungarian and German immigrant neighbourhoods, ending up at the far eastern edge of the island in a pocket of the Upper East Side with a very quiet, residential feel. The tour ends at Gracie Mansion, the city's official mayoral residence. If you would like to visit the mansion, reservations are needed and tours available only on Wednesdays.

Exit the N/R/W subway at the Fifth Avenue station, at 60th Street. Notice the Metropolitan Club's Fifth Avenue façade and the subtle 'M's' carved in the marble, but ultimately stand in front of the monumental gates and carriage entrance on 60th Street just east of Fifth Avenue, with the Harmonie Club across the street.

Those 'Ms' stand for Metropolitan, but they also could stand for J.P. Morgan, the force behind the creation of this club and its headquarters in 1891. When some of the more conservative members of the Union Club blackballed the admittance of Morgan's nouveau-riche friends, he decided to one-up them by building the most extravagant club in the city. During the Gilded Age, New York men conducted business (and dined, played cards and smoked cigars) behind the high walls of clubs. The clubs distinguished themselves by their amenities—the Metropolitan Club, for instance has a bowling alley—or their membership criteria—the Harmonie Club was for Germans. Stanford White, the architect of both these buildings, belonged to a score of clubs himself.

2 Continue to Madison Avenue, then turn left and walk two blocks to 62nd Street. Turn left for the Fabbri Mansion at 11 East 62nd Street.

Fifth Avenue was long regarded the most prestigious address in the city, and by the early 20th century the wealthiest families no longer had room to keep their sons and daughters nearby without moving them to the adjacent side streets. This house was the 1900 wedding present for Cornelius Vanderbilt's great-granddaughter when she married Count Ernesto Fabbri; note the decorative iron balconies with their 'F' monogram. With the coming of the apartment era, many of these side-street mansions (including this one) became home to non-profit organizations. More recently, this home was purchased by the Japanese government for its UN ambassador.

3 Continue on 62nd Street to Fifth Avenue, to see the Knickerbocker Club on the corner.

While J. P. Morgan may have founded the Metropolitan to protest against the Union Club's stringent admission

DISTANCE **3.1 miles (5km)**

ALLOW **1.75 hours**

START **Fifth Avenue station, N/R/W trains**

FINISH **86th Street station, 4/5/6 trains**

policies, the Knickerbocker Club was founded in 1871 by Union Club members who thought its admission policies were becoming too lenient. This 1915 Georgian Revival building by Delano and Aldrich embodies the club's rules of membership: One must—still to this day—prove colonial ancestry in order to belong. The term 'Knickerbocker' was coined by writer Washington Irving (best known as author of the chilling tale *The Legend of Sleepy Hollow*) to refer to the original Dutch settlers of Manhattan, though here there is no national restriction. (The word is best known today as the name of the city's professional basketball team, the Knicks.)

4 Walk three blocks north on Fifth Avenue to Temple Emanu-El.

Constructed in 1928 in a Moorish-meets-Art-Deco style, this is the grandest synagogue in the city. It also has the largest capacity of any house of worship in the city, with seating for over 2,500 in the main sanctuary. The interior features stunning mosaics by Hildreth Maier, but is not usually open for viewing.

5 Continue up Fifth Avenue to 66th Street, turn right and walk two blocks to Park Avenue.

Park Avenue now is synonymous with luxury, but originally trains running into Grand Central Terminal came down this street making it a loud, filthy thoroughfare. So, it was unusual for the wealthy Seventh Regiment to build their armory on this block between 66th and 67th Streets in 1879. The officer's room features Louis Comfort Tiffany mosaics. The ground floor remains one of the largest indoor spaces in the city, making it the perfect venue for antique shows. After 1903, when the railroad was forced below the street, Park Avenue prospered as one of the best addresses in the city.

6 Turn left onto Park Avenue and head north to 70th Street. At this point, those interested in more Fifth Avenue mansions can opt to leave this tour and begin Walk 17, 'The Architecture of Museum Mile', which starts right here at the Asia Society. To continue this tour, turn right onto 70th Street and walk three blocks east, passing some of the finest townhouses in the city. After this, you will be leaving the wealthier precincts of the Silk Stocking District and entering the immigrant neighbourhoods of Yorkville. Turn left onto Second Avenue. Walk three blocks north to 73rd Street and turn right to 321 East 73rd Street.

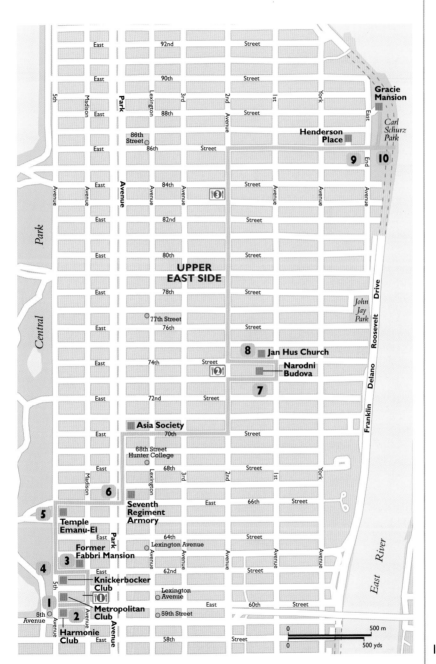

East 92nd Street

East 90th Street

5th · Madison · East · Park · Lexington · 3rd · East · 2nd · 1st · York

Gracie Mansion

East 88th Street

Carl Schurz Park

86th Street

86th Street

Henderson Place

9 **10**

East 84th Street · Avenue · **3**

East 82nd Street

East 80th Street

UPPER EAST SIDE

East 78th Street

77th Street

East 76th Street

Roosevelt Drive

John Jay Park

East 74th Street · **8** Jan Hus Church

Narodni Budova

7

East 72nd Street

Franklin · Delano

Asia Society

East 70th Street

68th Street Hunter College

East 68th Street · 3rd · 2nd · 1st · York

Lexington · Avenue

East 66th Street

6

East River

Seventh Regiment Armory

5

Temple Emanu-El

East 64th Street · Lexington Avenue

Former Fabbri Mansion

3

East 62nd Street

4

5th

Knickerbocker Club

Lexington Avenue

1

Park · Avenue

Metropolitan Club

East 60th Street

2

59th Street

5th Avenue

Madison · Avenue

Harmonie Club

East 58th Street

0   500 m
0   500 yds

WHERE TO EAT

🍴 FRED'S AT BARNEYS NEW YORK, 660 Madison Avenue (at 61st Street); Tel: 212-833-2200.
Italian and American food amidst high-priced fashion splendour.

🍴 SLICE—THE PERFECT FOOD, 1413 Second Avenue (between 73rd and 74th Streets);
Tel: 212-249-4353.
Custom-made pizza using unusual and/or organic ingredients.

🍴 JACKSON HOLE, 1611 Second Avenue (between 83rd and 84th Streets);
Tel: 212-737-8788.
Americana-themed burger joint; great retro jukebox.

The Bohemian National Hall or 'Narodni Budova' was, in the early days of the 20th century, the most important Czech-American building in the country, providing immigrant services, social events and playing host to the most famous Czech in New York, composer Antonin Dvorák, who led the Academy of Music downtown. After years of neglect, the building is undergoing a thorough restoration to eventually house the Czech Consulate.

7 Continue east on 73rd Street to First Avenue, then turn left and walk one block to 74th Street. Turn left again for the Jan Hus Church.

Jan Hus, a 15th-century Czech priest who was excommunicated and burned at the stake for his radical ideas, was a later influence on the Reformation, in particular Martin Luther. This church was founded to serve the Czech and Hungarian communities that were filling up the neighbourhood in the last decades of the 19th century. For years, neighbours thought the building was haunted, for they kept hearing what sounded like a wolf howling from the belfry. It turned out it was a black wolf that the pastor kept as a pet. It lived in the church and often slept in the pulpit.

8 Continue west to Second Avenue. Turn right and walk 12 blocks north to 86th Street. You will pass stores and restaurants that are reminders of Yorkville's Hungarian and German populations. At 86th Street, turn right and walk three blocks east to Henderson Place.

These charming Queen Anne homes were built by developer John Henderson and architects Lamb & Rich to be homes for, in Henderson's words, 'persons of moderate means'. Twenty-four of the original 32 homes remain; they are smaller than average townhouses—usually 18 by 46ft (5.5 by 14m)—but that did not stop them from becoming a desirable address as New York's fashionable elite moved into the far East Side in the 1920s.

9 Cross East End Avenue into Carl Schurz Park and walk on any path to the water's edge.

Named after the German-American publisher, statesman and military commander Carl Schurz, this park bordering the river provides excellent views across to Wards Island (to the north), Roosevelt Island (south) and Queens. The particularly treacherous current here was called by the Dutch 'Hell Gate' and is the result not only of the confluence of the East and Harlem Rivers but also the great difference between high and low tide at opposite ends of this strait.

10 Walk within the park to Gracie Mansion, at 88th Street.

Built in 1799 by merchant Archibald Gracie—5 miles (8km) north of what was then the northern border of New York—this is a rare surviving example of an 18th-century country estate. Formerly a museum, the mansion has been the official home of New York City's Mayor since the 1940s when Fiorello LaGuardia moved in.

GRACIE MANSION; TOURS ON WED BY RESERVATION ONLY;

TEL: 212-639-9675 (the city's information line)
For the nearest subway, retrace your steps back to 86th Street and walk to Lexington Avenue for the 4/5/6 train at the 86th Street station.

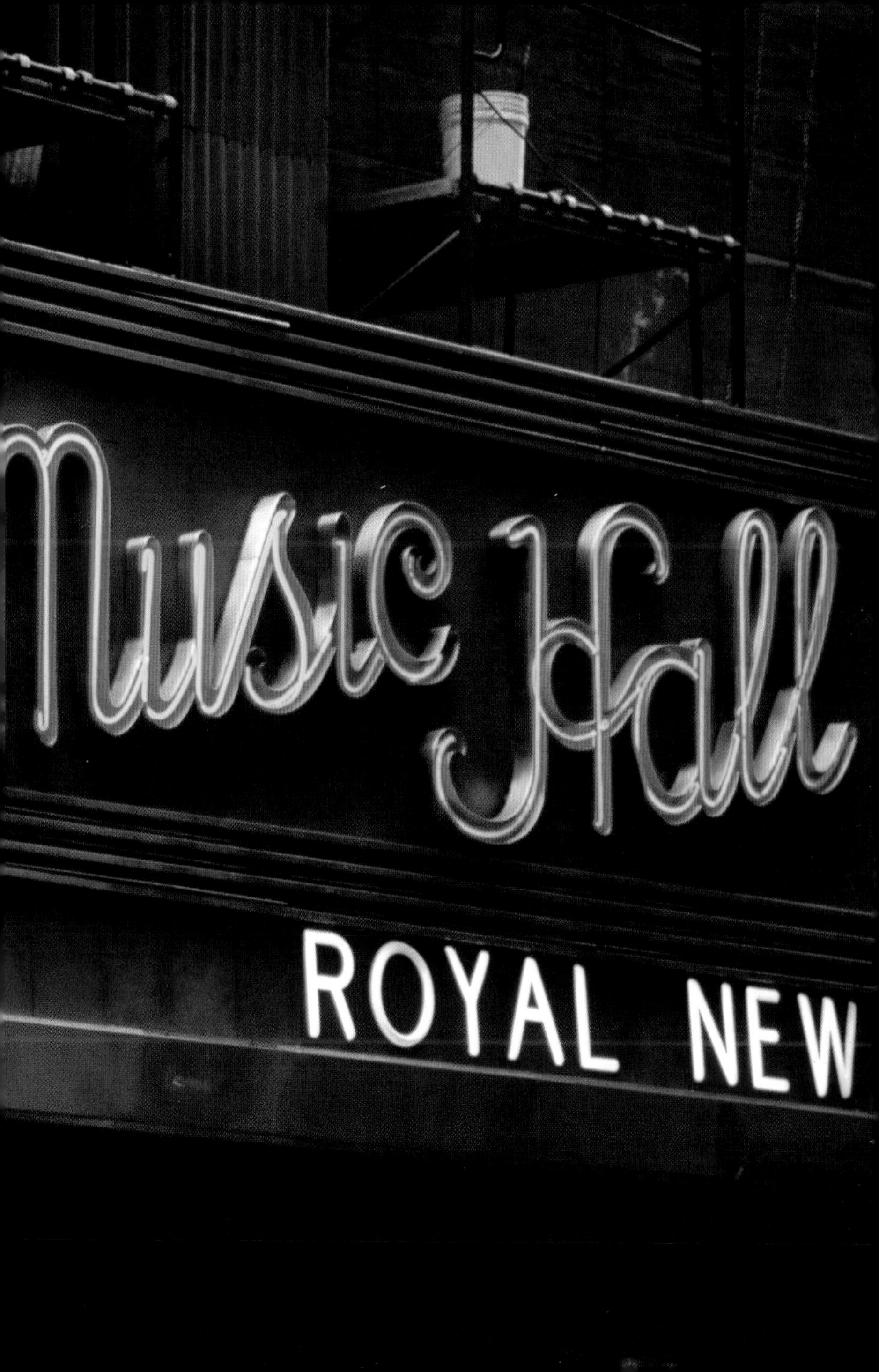
Music Hall
ROYAL NEW

The Architecture of Museum Mile

Many of New York's museums, from the all-encompassing Metropolitan to the intimate Neue Gallerie, are housed on elegant Fifth Avenue.

New York is America's reigning cultural capital, but in the 19th century this was hardly the case. The city had few museums and, until the opening of the Metropolitan Museum in 1869, there was little public access to great art. By contrast, New York's mercantile elite were acquiring vast amounts of art to show off in private galleries for their own enjoyment and that of their friends. This tour brings together both worlds; it provides a glimpse—in spaces like the Frick Collection—into the way art was collected in the Gilded Age as well as displaying the philanthropic spirit of institutions like the Met and of wealthy New Yorkers such as Gertrude Vanderbilt Whitney and Ronald Lauder. The tour is designed so that you can enjoy each museum from the outside simply for its architectural merit. Half of the museums on the route were once mansions; the others were created specifically to house art. If you build in time to venture inside any of the museums as you go, this tour could also easily take a full day.

Exit the 6 subway at 68th Street. Walk north on Lexington Avenue to 70th Street. Turn left and walk one block west to the Asia Society.

This 1981 building—an unusually modern structure for Park Avenue—is by Edward Larabee Barnes and was recently completely renovated inside by Voorsanger & Associates. The society was founded in 1956 by John D. Rockefeller III both to continue his father's interest in fostering East-West relations and to showcase his impressive array of South Asian and Oriental art and antiques.

ASIA SOCIETY;

TUE–SUN 11–6 (OPEN FRI UNTIL 9);
TEL: 212-288-6400; www.asiasociety.org

2 Continue west on 70th Street to the corner of Fifth Avenue and the Frick Collection. The expanse of the building is best seen from Fifth Avenue.

Andrew Carnegie's protégé-turned-rival, coal baron Henry Clay Frick, moved to New York from Pittsburgh to showcase his art collection, one of the finest in America. Frick demolished the Lenox Library, which had recently been subsumed into the New York Public Library, and hired Thomas Hastings to build this mansion in its place. Hastings had orders to make Carnegie's home on 93rd Street 'look like a miner's shack'. It was Frick's intent that the space would ultimately be opened to the public. When his wife Adelaide died in 1935, art dealer Joseph Duveen oversaw the transformation. Across Fifth Avenue sits

Daniel Chester French's bust of architect Richard Morris Hunt, placed here to face the Lenox Library, a magnificent Hunt building. Within a decade of the memorial's installation, the Lenox mansion was gone, and Hunt now looks forlornly across at someone else's work.

FRICK COLLECTION;

TUE–SAT 10–6, SUN 11–5; TEL: 212-288-0700;
www.frick.org

3 Walk north along Fifth Avenue to 71st Street. Turn right and walk one block to Madison Avenue, then turn left and head four blocks north to the Whitney Museum of American Art.

By 1929, artist and heiress Gertrude Vanderbilt Whitney had a collection of over 600 works of art by contemporary American artists, many of them from her Greenwich Village circle of friends, such as John Sloan and Edward Hopper. When her small exhibition space in the Village became too crowded, she offered her

DISTANCE **2.5 miles (4 km)**

ALLOW **1.5 hours**

START **68th Street station, 6 train**

FINISH **103rd Street station, 6 train**

collection (and the wing to house it) to the Metropolitan and was turned down. The Whitney's current home, by Marcel Breuer, opened in this inverted ziggurat in 1966.

THE WHITNEY MUSEUM OF AMERICAN ART;
WED–THU 11–6, FRI 1–9, SAT–SUN 11–6;
TEL: 212-570-3600; www.whitney.org

4 Walk four blocks north on Madison Avenue. Turn left onto 79th Street and walk to Fifth Avenue and the Ukrainian Institute of America.

Architect C.P.H. Gilbert built this home for Isaac D. and Mary Fletcher in 1899 to resemble a chateau in the Loire Valley. It was sold to oil baron Harry F. Sinclair and, later, to the last living direct descendant of Peter Stuyvesant. Since the 1950s, it has housed the Ukrainian Institute, which hosts temporary exhibitions. Gilbert's style is flamboyant and rich in detail. Notice the pairs of sour-faced rustic figures flanking the entry along with dragons and other animals in the detail.

UKRAINIAN INSTITUTE OF AMERICA;
TEL: 212-288-8660; www.ukrainianinstitute.org

5 Walk three blocks north up Fifth Avenue to the Metropolitan Museum of Art.

America's pre-eminent art museum opened (elsewhere) in 1869 with a small collection of Dutch and Flemish paintings. As Central Park neared completion, the city granted the Metropolitan a prime location; Calvert Vaux and Jacob Wrey Mould constructed the museum's first home on this site, oriented to face the park. Tremendous growth in the 20th century resulted in numerous additions, the most important of which shifted the entrance to Richard Morris Hunt's Fifth Avenue façade. (Even the Met isn't immune to funding problems—note the pyramids of uncarved stone above the colonnade.) An interior exploration of the Met is a worthwhile addition to the tour. The façade of Vaux and Mould's original building is visible from the Lehman wing and the European Sculpture Court adjoins Theodore Weston's 1888 addition to the museum. In addition, one entrance to the American Wing is the front of the old Bank of the United States and nearby, a period room recreates a fabulous Frank Lloyd Wright home.

METROPOLITAN MUSEUM OF ART;
TUE–THU AND SUN 9.30–5.30, FRI–SAT 9.30–9;
TEL: 212-535-7710; www.metmuseum.org

6 Walk four blocks north on Fifth Avenue to reach the intimate Neue Gallerie.

Conservatory
Garden

East 106th Street

East 104th Street

**Museum of the
City of New York**

103rd Street

East 102nd Street

E 100th St   E 100th St

East 98th Street

96th Street

East 96th Street

10

East 94th Street

East 92nd Street

**Cooper-Hewitt
National Design Museum**

9

Central
Park
Reservoir

East 90th Street

**Guggenheim
Museum**

8

East 88th Street

86th Street Transverse Road

86th Street

86th Street

7

⌂ **Neue Gallerie**   **UPPER EAST
SIDE**

East 84th Street

**Metropolitan
Museum of Art**

81st Street
Museum of
Nat Hist

Great
Lawn

6

East 82nd Street

Central
Park

East 80th Street

5

79th Street Transverse Road

**Ukrainian
Institute of
America**

East 78th Street

77th
Street

The
Ramble

East 76th Street

**Whitney Museum
of American Art**

4

East 74th Street

The
Lake

⌂

East 72nd Street

72nd
Street

Olmsted Drive

**Frick
Collection**

3

⌂ **Asia Society**

East 70th Street

The Sheep
Meadow

2

68th Street
Hunter College

East 68th Street

I

123

The Neue Gallerie, dedicated to German and Austrian art and design, is Museum Mile's newest addition. The home, built by Carrère & Hastings in 1914 for William Starr Miller, was later owned by Mrs Cornelius Vanderbilt. The museum's small permanent collection provides a telling contrast to its setting: Carrère & Hastings bombastic French palace is decidedly 17th century, while the objects in the Neue Gallerie's collection from the same period are modern, prefiguring later Deco and Minimalist designs.

NEUE GALLERIE;
SAT–MON AND THU 11–6, FRI 11–9;
TEL: 212-628-6200; www.neuegallerie.org

7 Walk two blocks north up Fifth Avenue to the Guggenheim Museum.

This is the only major Frank Lloyd Wright building in New York and, completed in 1959, his last large-scale work. It is also among the most important museum spaces in the world. Wright himself described this as the building that 'destroys everything square, rectilinear'. Its best feature is the triumphant spiral of the main exhibition space, a ¼ mile (400m) of unbroken ramp that twists down from the skylight and provides startling lines of sight across the open atrium. The interior is always worth a visit, but is often best when showing 20th- and 21st-century art.

GUGGENHEIM MUSEUM;
SAT–WED 10–5.45, FRI 10–7.45;
TEL: 212-423-3500; www.guggenheim.org

8 Walk three blocks north to the Cooper-Hewitt National Design Museum.

Babb, Cook & Willard finished this 'modest' (to use Carnegie's words) home for steel magnate Andrew Carnegie in 1903. Carnegie also wanted it to be 'roomy'—with 64 rooms and only three inhabitants, he undoubtedly got his wish.

Since 1968, it has housed the Cooper-Hewitt National Design Museum. Even when exhibitions crowd the walls, the interiors still reveal lavish original details—this is truly the grandest house-museum on Fifth Avenue.

COOPER-HEWITT NATIONAL DESIGN MUSEUM;
MON-THU 10–5, FRI 10–9, SAT 10–6, SUN 12–6; TEL: 212-849-8400; www.cooperhewitt.org

9 Continue three blocks north to 1130 Fifth Avenue.

This Georgian Revival mansion was completed in 1915 by Delano & Aldrich for Willard Straight; he didn't have long to appreciate it as three years later he died in the worldwide flu pandemic. It was converted into public space and for years housed the International Center for Photography, but in 2000 was sold to a private owner for $17.5 million.

10 Walk nine blocks north up Fifth Avenue to the Museum of the City of New York.

Completed in 1932, architect Joseph Freedlander attempted to provide sympathetic design and context for the mansion-filled streetscape of Fifth Avenue. Statues of two great New Yorkers face the street: Alexander Hamilton (left), America's first Treasury Secretary, and DeWitt Clinton (right), New York's unsung hero. As governor, Clinton had the Erie Canal built, thus connecting the country's interior to the Atlantic via New York. He also, as the city's mayor,

WHERE TO EAT

🍴 GARDEN COURT CAFÉ,
in the Asia Society;
725 Park Avenue (at 70th Street);
Tel: 212-570-5202.
Pan-asian tea in a fabulous glass atrium; closed Mon.

🍴 VIA QUADRONNO,
25 East 73rd Street
(at Madison Avenue);
Tel: 212-650-9880.
Reasonably priced Italian food in an area not normally known for bargain dining.

🍴 CAFÉ SABARSKY,
in the Neue Gallerie;
1048 Fifth Avenue (at 86th Street);
Tel: 212-288-0665.
Viennese coffee house; its cousin—Café Fledermaus downstairs—usually has a shorter wait; closed Tue.

commissioned the grid plan of streets and kept the city out of the War of 1812, which would have proven economically ruinous. Just north is the entrance to Central Park's Conservatory Gardens. These French, Italianate and English gardens, often the site of elegant wedding photos, are a great place to relax.

MUSEUM OF THE CITY OF NEW YORK;
TUE–SUN 10–5; TEL: 212-534-1672; www.mcny.org
Turn onto 102nd Street, cross Park Avenue and turn left into Lexington Avenue for 103rd Street station.

Landscape Versus Playground

This walk through magnificent Central Park focuses on its attempts to bring nature into the city and provide entertainment for its users.

Central Park, created by architects Frederick Law Olmsted and Calvert Vaux and built between 1857 and 1873, is America's premier urban park and one of the grandest pieces of landscape architecture ever created. It encompasses 843 acres, stretching from 59th to 110th Street and from Fifth Avenue to Eighth Avenue. The park's initial purpose was to provide a respite for the congestion of the city—which then barely reached above 14th Street—and to give the city's largely immigrant working class access to the beauty of nature. Early on, however, it became apparent that landscape alone would not be enough to draw poorer New Yorkers to the park and tensions grew over its purpose—was it simply enough to provide beautifully crafted outdoor space, or did the city need to supply entertainment as well? This tour examines the tensions between landscaping and fun; its companion tour, 'From the Castle to the Woods', explores its more picturesque landscape designs.

Exit the N/R/W subway at Fifth Avenue and walk four blocks north to enter the park at 64th Street.

This ornate arsenal once housed munitions—note the banisters held up by rifles and other militant decorations. Five years after the building opened, however, it found itself annexed into Central Park. Olmsted and Vaux considered keeping it as a picturesque folly; instead, it became the home of the park's first zoo. (A zoo became necessary when patrons began donating animals to the park—ignoring the fact that the plans made no provisions for them!) The animals later moved into a menagerie (today a fine small wildlife centre) and this building served as the home of the Museum of Natural History. Today it is the headquarters of New York City's Parks Department.

WHERE TO EAT

[IOI] LEAPING FROG CAFÉ,
at the Central Park Zoo;
Tel: 212-717-8918.
Wide range of selections in a family-friendly environment.

[IOI] TAVERN ON THE GREEN,
in Central Park at 67th Street on the West Side;
Tel: 212-873-3200.
Dine in the Tiffany-glass makeover of what was once Central Park's barn.

[IOI] SAMBUCA,
20 W 72nd Street
(near Central Park West);
Tel: 212-787-5656.
Southern Italian cuisine served family style.

2 Walk behind the arsenal, where you'll see the present zoo. Facing the zoo, with the arsenal at your back, take the path heading left (south)—away from the decorative Delacorte Clock. You will pass the Leaping Frog Café and then head out of the zoo's south gates. Immediately to your right, you'll see an arched stone underpass. Go through it to emerge at the pond.

All the bodies of water in the park are artificial, which allowed Olmsted and Vaux to manipulate their decorative water features. In fact, in its early years, most park visitors came in winter when the Pond could be drained to a depth of a few inches and would thus freeze for skating. Once technology allowed for the construction of skating rinks, a portion of the pond was demolished and converted into Wollman Rink.

3 Walk north along the edge of the pond, keeping the water on your left, to come to Wollman Rink. The ice rink is operational from mid-October through mid-April; in mid-summer you may see a small amusement park set up here. Continue past the Wollman rink. You will see the ornate Victorian Dairy building on your right, at the top of a small hill. At the first opportunity, take a path on your right (up the hill), to get to the Dairy.

OPPOSITE: WOLLMAN RINK

DISTANCE **2 miles (3.2 km)**

ALLOW **1 hour**

START **Fifth Avenue station, N/R/W trains**

FINISH **72nd Street, B/C trains**

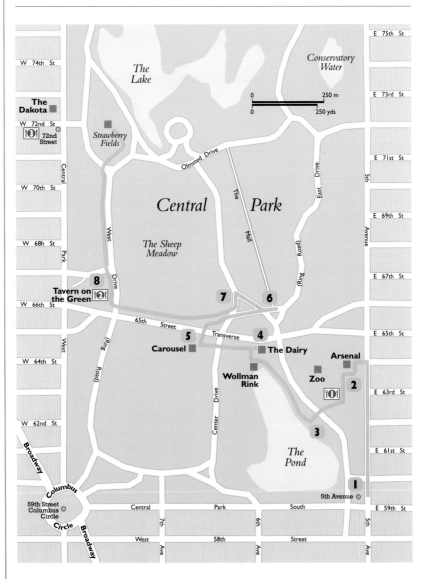

As Olmsted and Vaux's work on Central Park progressed, it became clear that truly serving New York's immigrant population would require more than simply inviting them to the park to enjoy nature's bounty. They created a children's district with this Dairy at its heart. Stocked with cows milked by costumed milkmaids, it was to provide free, healthy milk to children. Alas, budgetary concerns forced the Dairy to open as a restaurant instead (sans cows or milkmaids). Today, it is the park's visitor centre and gift shop.

4 From the Dairy's porch, look south back towards Wollman Rink. Turn right and walk past the Chess and Checkers pavilion (on your left) and under a beautiful yellow-and-red brick underpass to the carousel.

Another highlight of the children's district was a carousel, one of the first paid amusements in the park. The original was hand-cranked, then manual labour was replaced by a horse tethered to a mechanism in the basement. When the carousel burned down in the 1950s, it was replaced by this magnificent 1908 merry-go-round imported from an amusement park at Coney Island. The horses are hand carved by the firm Stein & Goldstein, long considered the greatest carousel artists in America.

CENTRAL PARK CAROUSEL;
Tel: 212-879-0244

5 Keeping the carousel on your left, walk up the hill. You are now walking next to the 'ring road', the old carriage drive that makes a 6-mile (9.66-km) circuit of the park. Keeping the ring road on your right, walk until you can see a statue of Christopher Columbus on your left. Go to the Columbus statue and walk past him to the foot of the Mall, where a compass rose is embedded in the pavement.

Olmsted and Vaux's design emphasized naturalism. In fact, one reason why they beat the other entrants in the park's design competition was their emphasis on pastoral asymmetry, not rigid formality. But here on the Mall, all pretense of naturalism gives way to a broad, Parisian walkway. This grove of elm trees is the largest remaining in North America after the decimation of Dutch elm disease in the 1920s. The Mall's formality stems not only from being the park's only straight path, but also from its central position, drawing visitors due north towards the heart of the park. Early in the park's life, this was a favoured spot for statuary; four of the five men depicted here are poets (Shakespeare, Burns, Scott and little-known American Halleck), earning it the nickname 'Literary Walk'. The fifth statue, Columbus, was erected in 1894 following the commemorations of the 400th anniversary of his voyage to America.

6 Standing on the compass rose and facing north, look left (through the trees) to see a statue of a man and his dog—*The Indian Hunter* by J.Q.A Ward (who also sculpted Shakespeare). Walk to that statue and beyond it to the fence surrounding the Sheep Meadow.

In the original scheme of the park, this was to have been a militia drilling area and public parade. However, during the Civil War, Olmsted and Vaux converted the area to a Sheep Meadow instead, which was more consistent with their overall pastoral vision. Southdown sheep were installed in 1864 and a flock was a feature of the park until 1934.

7 Your next stop is on the opposite side of the Sheep Meadow. Facing west—you'll see twin towered apartment buildings, such as the San Remo and Majestic—begin walking along the Sheep Meadow towards the west side. As you walk, you'll *always have the meadow's tall fence on your right.* When you reach the ring road on the far side of the meadow, you cross the road to Tavern on the Green. *Be careful as you cross the road—joggers and bikers have right of way at all times.*

Built in 1870, this was originally the sheepfold (the first sections, with Victorian Gothic layered stone and

brick, were built by Olmsted and Vaux's assistant, Jacob Wrey Mould). In 1934, the sheep were banished, ostensibly because the small flock was inbreeding. In reality, the sheep were exiled to free up this building to become Tavern on the Green. The park's popular restaurant, the Casino, had been an elitist speakeasy throughout Prohibition. Populist Mayor Fiorello LaGuardia wanted to clean up the city's image and had the Casino torn down. The sheep were exiled, their barn renovated, and this restaurant opened.

8 From Tavern on the Green, head north, keeping the ring road on your right. Just before you reach Strawberry Fields (in approximately five minutes), an exit from the ring road will climb the hill to your left. Cross this road and you'll see a sign on your left that reads 'Strawberry Fields'. At the sign, take either path to go up the hill to the *Imagine* mosaic.

Soon after John Lennon's murder in December 1980, New York's City Council voted to commemorate the slain musician with a field of strawberries. Over 160 countries donated plants and an Italian artist created the mosaic *Imagine*. It attracts scores of visitors each year. To see the Dakota, Lennon's apartment, exit here and begin Walk 20 – 'New York's Last Frontier'. To begin the other Central Park tour, 'From the Castle to the Woods', walk north on Central Park West to 81st Street. The nearest subway is the B/C station at the corner of 72nd Street and Central Park West.

MANHATTAN

From the Castle to the Woods

Central Park has been called a landscape painting brought to life. In this walk, natural elements combine with architecture to create a work of art. Central Park's designers, Frederick Law Olmsted and Calvert Vaux, were chosen for a plan that combined pastoral, formal and picturesque elements. Heirs to the landscape theory of designers such as Capability Brown, the team (particularly Olmsted) believed that walking through Central Park should be like walking into a painting, with every possible variety of naturalistic setting on display. This meant the construction of calm, idyllic lakes, sweeping green meadows, thickly wooded areas—and landscape follies, such as rustic shelters and, at one of the park's highest peaks, a miniature castle. This walk explores some of the park's most picturesque landscape features; its companion tour, 'Landscape Versus Playground', examines some of the challenges that were faced by the designers in creating a park that people would actually use.

Exit the B/C subway at 81st Street at Central Park West and enter the park on the path just north of 81st Street. Keep right to follow that path until it reaches the park's main road. This is known as the 'ring road' and is the place where joggers, bikers and, during the morning rush-hour, cars circle the park. Cross the road here and turn right to the small wooden house. *Be careful—joggers and bikers have right of way at all times and do not stop for pedestrians.*

Though most of Central Park's rustic buildings were planned by Olmsted and Vaux, the city also accepted gifts, including this cottage used as the Swedish pavilion at the 1876 Centennial Exposition in Philadelphia. It is now a marionette theatre.

2 Take the path next to the cottage to the Shakespeare Garden that lies behind it.

Planted as a study garden in 1915, the Shakespeare Garden is home to over 100 species mentioned by the Bard, many of which were at that time unknown to Americans. The variety of flowers ensures that something is in bloom from mid-March until the end of the year. The same impetus drove a businessman to release starlings in Central Park in 1890—they were mentioned in Shakespeare but unseen in North America. Every pesky starling in the US descends from that Central Park flock.

WHERE TO EAT

🍽 KERBS ICE CREAM CAFÉ, at Conservatory Water at 74th Street; no telephone. Eat ice cream and watch the model boats go by.

🍽 BOATHOUSE CENTRAL PARK, on the Lake at 74th Street; Tel: 212-517-2233. Pricey, but the view is great. Also a takeaway café.

3 Walk through the Shakespeare Garden to reach the top of the hill. A path in front of you leads up to Belvedere Castle.

Vaux designed this castle as the park's primary landscape folly. It is both a picturesque companion to the wooded Ramble below and a contrast to the more formal Bethesda Terrace. Indeed, when the castle was completed in 1869, its turret could be seen from Bethesda Terrace, with which it is perfectly aligned. The National Weather Service has a monitoring station here and on top of the turret you can see their equipment. Stand at the edge and look north. Directly below is Turtle Pond and beyond that the Great Lawn, a 1930s addition to the park created when the old Croton Reservoir was torn down. This is the site of large open-air concerts, although gatherings of more than 70,000 people are currently restricted.

OPPOSITE: BETHESDA TERRACE

135

DISTANCE 2 miles (3.2 km)

ALLOW 1 hour

START 81st Street station, B/C trains

FINISH 72nd Street, B/C trains

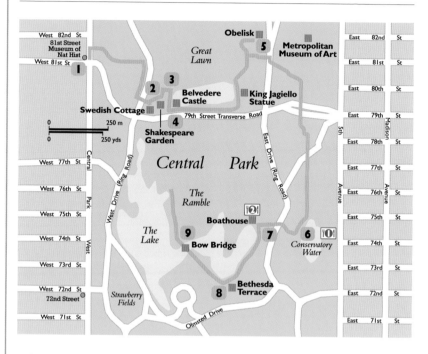

4 With the entrance to Belvedere Castle to your left, walk down the sloping pathway ahead of you and to the left. (Don't go straight towards the black cage of weather equipment.) You'll see Turtle Pond to your left as you walk. When you reach the large equestrian statue of King Jagiello labelled POLAND, turn left to walk in front of it and follow the path down the hill (not towards the Great Lawn) until it brings you to an almost hidden small flight of steps, on your right, that lead to the obelisk.

Just as it was beginning to remake itself in the style of a European city, New York decided it needed an Egyptian obelisk. Railroad baron William Henry Vanderbilt paid to have this one—the sister of London's and nicknamed 'Cleopatra's Needle'—brought here from Alexandria. First, it had to be removed from its pedestal in Egypt, no small feat for a 270 ton (244,940kg) piece of rock. After ferrying it across the Atlantic, a special railway conveyed it from the Hudson River to the park. It took 111 days.

5 From the obelisk, go down the steps to the main path and turn left. Make an immediate left to go under Greywacke Arch. Once you are through the arch (with the Metropolitan Museum in front of you), take the right fork, keeping the museum on your left. At the first opportunity turn right and walk straight. You'll pass Cedar Hill and come to an underpass. Go through it and continue straight for another minute or two to the Conservatory Water.

In the original plan, the Conservatory Water was intended to be the centre of the park's formal flower garden, but because the money for the garden was shunted to other projects, the pond ended up standing alone. (The garden did eventually open, at 105th Street.) For years, this has been known as the Model Boat Pond, and on sunny days it is filled with a flotilla of radio-controlled yachts. Serious boaters can berth their models in the small green-roofed building on the pond's Fifth Avenue side. Two statues enliven the area: George Lober's *Hans Christian Andersen* (complete with ugly duckling) and *Alice in Wonderland* by Jose de Creeft.

6 Facing the statue of Hans Christian Andersen (opposite the Model Boat house), take the path to the left which comes to a dead end almost immediately. Curve to the right and soon you'll see the large Trefoil Arch ahead of you and to the left. Pass under the arch, climb the stairs and you will be at the Boathouse and the Lake.

The Lake, the largest of Olmsted and Vaux's picturesque bodies of water, has always been used recreationally. Once popular, ice skating is no longer allowed, in order to preserve the park's ecology. Today, the main activity is boating ($12 per hour), but the Boathouse also serves as a café, restaurant and serene outdoor bar. Occasionally, you'll see the gondolier punting lucky guests around the lake and singing arias.

7 Keeping the lake on your right, walk from the Boathouse (past the rowboats) to Bethesda Terrace.

Bethesda Terrace is the formal heart of the park and one of the most majestic public spaces in New York. The bulk of the design is by Vaux's assistant, Jacob Wrey Mould, who took the park's ideas of changing nature as his overall aesthetic plan. Note the vegetative designs of the main staircases—each balustrade represents a season and each plant is different from its neighbours. Underneath the arcade, there is the painstakingly rebuilt Minton tile ceiling. At the terrace's centre is the *Angel of the Waters* by Emma Stebbins (1872), the first work of public art by a female artist in New York. The statue represents the healing power of water and serves as a memorial for the Union naval dead from the Civil War.

8 Facing the *Angel of the Waters* and the Lake, you will see two paths coming in from the left. Take the path closest to the lake and follow it around to Bow Bridge.

This cast-iron suspension bridge from 1862 was one of the first architectural elements added to the park and it quickly became a focal point. However, it was not without controversy. Frederick Law Olmsted, in particular, purportedly didn't like the idea of a piece of decorative architecture ruining the long vista across the Lake, nor did he want walkers to have a shortcut from the terrace to the wooded Ramble beyond. The bridge's popularity soon made it a symbol of the park and it is still shown in countless TV shows, movies and photographs.

9 Cross Bow Bridge into the Ramble. Keeping the lake on your left, follow the path for a minute or so until you reach a rustic wooded bridge over the small stream that feeds the lake.

As the name suggests, this was the part of the park designed for rambling and

was planted in such a way as to appear completely wild. This small stream, called the Gill, originates in the heart of the Ramble, but if you were to follow it up to its source, you'd find a large valve. Like everything else in the park, it is manmade, and it is a fine example of how Vaux and Olmsted meticulously crafted the landscape to be a living work of art.

The best way to exit the park from here is to retrace your steps to Bethesda Terrace. When you climb the grand staircase, it brings you to the 72nd Street Transverse road. Turn right (west) and follow the road to the corner of 72nd Street and Central Park West and the B/C subway.

If, however, you'd like to start the other Central Park tour, turn left onto the 72nd Street Transverse and follow it in the other direction to Fifth Avenue. Walk down Fifth Avenue to 64th Street and the first stop on that tour.

BOATHOUSE RESTAURANT

New York's Last Frontier

Chart a course across the Upper West Side from the Dakota—New York's first real luxury apartment building—to the wilds of Riverside Park.

The completion of Central Park in the 1870s forever changed New York real estate, not least because it created an Upper East Side and an Upper West Side separated by the 0.5 mile (805m) gulf of the park. The two neighbourhoods developed in markedly different ways: the Upper East Side, settled first, came to define status in the city and the buildings along Fifth Avenue facing the park still have the highest property values. The west side, by contrast, was virtually the countryside until the opening of the Dakota apartment building, which in turn led to the creation of smart residential streets such as West End Avenue and Riverside Drive. Riverside Park was completed by the end of the 19th century, meaning that no Upper West Side resident is ever more than two blocks from park land, a factor which still lends an air of tranquillity to the neighbourhood to this day. Most importantly, the success of the Dakota sparked the development of the luxury apartment building, which within 50 years replaced the townhouse and mansion as the preferred mode of living in the city.

Exit the B/C subway at 72nd Street and, for the best view of the yellow-brick Dakota, cross to Central Park.

It's often said that when developer Edward Clark announced he was building apartments on 72nd Street, someone joked, 'You might as well build it in the Dakotas' and the name stuck. In truth, Clark fully understood his tenants would be pioneers in the then-underdeveloped Upper West Side. (Clark also backed a plan to rename nearby avenues after western states. While this never happened, avenue names *do* change on the west side—Eighth Avenue is Central Park West, Ninth Avenue is Columbus, etc.) When it opened in 1884, what made the Dakota groundbreaking (apart from its location) was its luxury. For generations, New York's social hierarchy dictated that the poor could live in tenements, but everyone else—except, perhaps, bachelors and artists—owned a home. The Dakota, designed by Henry Hardenbergh, upended this notion, advertising the amenities of apartment life without the hassles of home ownership. The most famous resident of the Dakota was John Lennon, who was murdered below the twin gas lamps on 8 December 1980 by deranged fan Mark David Chapman. Look across 72nd Street at the twin-towered Majestic, completed in 1930. When the Dakota opened, this was a farm. One of the Majestic's carpenters was Bruno Hauptmann, who was later executed for kidnapping Charles Lindbergh's infant son. The bulk of the $50,000 ransom paid by Lindbergh is

WHERE TO EAT

🍽 EDGAR'S CAFÉ,
255 West 84th Street (between Broadway and West End Avenue);
Tel: 212-496-6126.
Coffee and full menu on the spot where Poe once lived.

🍽 ZABAR'S CAFÉ,
2245 Broadway (at 80th Street);
Tel: 212-787-2000.
Take-away attached to NYC's most famous gourmet market.

🍽 RUBY FOO'S,
2182 Broadway
(between 77th and 78th Streets);
Tel: 212-724-6700.
Glitzy Asian fare but with a neighbourhood feel.

thought by some to be stashed behind a wall somewhere in the building.

2 Walk north on Central Park West to 73rd Street to view the San Remo, which stands one block north, between 74th and 75th Streets.

The San Remo vies with the Dakota and Beresford (on 81st Street) for the title of best address on the park. Designed by Emery Roth in 1930, it makes use of new zoning regulations to increase light and decrease bulk. The towers taper at the top to replicate the ancient Lysicrates monument in Athens, a favourite source for Neoclassical designers.

141

DISTANCE 2 miles (3.2 km)

ALLOW 1 hour

START 72nd Street station, B/C trains

FINISH 86th Street station, 1 train

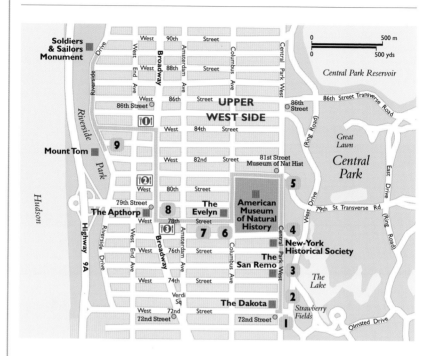

3 Walk north on Central Park West to 77th Street. On the south side stands the New-York Historical Society.

The New-York Historical Society was the city's first museum. Founded in 1804 (when New York was hyphenated), the society's collection of early Americana is unmatched, with over 40,000 objects on view in its study galleries alone. The society moved to this building in 1908.
NEW-YORK HISTORICAL SOCIETY;
TEL: 212-873-3400; www.nyhistory.org

4 Continue north on Central Park West to 81st Street, passing the main entrance to the American Museum of Natural History.

Planned as a companion to the Metropolitan Museum of Art, the museum's original building—buried beneath multiple later additions—is by Calvert Vaux and Jacob Wrey Mould and when the museum opened in 1877, it was the only structure of note on the west side. This grand entrance, added in 1936,

faces Central Park and—if contemporary plans had prevailed—would have been the culmination of a wide boulevard through the park. The new entrance glorifies US President Roosevelt, shown here in an equestrian statue by James Earl Fraser. Roosevelt was an ardent museum supporter and, as the only born-and-bred New Yorker to be president, inspired many memorials following his death in 1919. The museum houses millions of artifacts, including the world's largest repository of dinosaur bones.

AMERICAN MUSEUM OF NATURAL HISTORY; DAILY 10–5.45; TEL: 212-769-5100; www.amnh.org

5 Walk east on 81st Street to Columbus Avenue, noting on the way the recently added Rose Center for Earth and Space, a state-of-the-art planetarium. At Columbus Avenue, turn left and walk three blocks to 78th Street. As you walk along, you will see parts of Vaux and Mould's original Victorian Gothic brick-and-stone façade peeking through the later additions at the rear of the museum. Cross Columbus Avenue at 78th Street to the Evelyn apartments.

This red-brick structure opened in 1886 as a private hotel for the wealthy Thaw family of Pittsburgh. Harry K. Thaw married showgirl Evelyn Nesbit, who had once had an affair with architect Stanford White. Insanely jealous of White, Thaw decided to protect his wife's honour by murdering White in the rooftop theatre of Madison Square Garden in 1906. After the trial, in which Thaw was sentenced to a sanitarium, it is said that Evelyn retired to this building, which was later named after her. However, some evidence points to the building carrying the name Evelyn from its inception, when Nesbit would have been only two years old.

6 Continue west to 121-131 West 78th Street.

These 1886 buildings by Valencian architect Rafael Guastavino stand out in this eclectic block of townhouses. Guastavino is better known for his unique ceramic tile work, used to great effect in the ceilings of such diverse places as the Oyster Bar at Grand Central Terminal and the crossing of the Cathedral of St John the Divine. However, unlike these homes, Guastavino's later work doesn't reveal the same Moorish influence of his homeland.

7 Continue west on 78th Street one-and-a-half blocks to Broadway to see the Apthorp building.

What began with the Dakota in 1884 reached an apex with the giant, full-block Apthorp in 1908, designed by Clinton & Russell and built by William Waldorf Astor. All apartments were ten rooms or larger and the grand courtyard allowed light into the normally dark interiors. Among the building's amenities were porcelain-lined refrigerators (served by a central cooling plant, not ice) and a rooftop promenade.

8 Proceed north six blocks on Broadway to 84th Street. On the way, you will find yourself walking through the commercial hub of the Upper West Side. Turn left and walk two blocks west to Riverside Drive. Cross to the park side of the street and walk slightly south (left) to view the outcrop of rock known as Mount Tom.

Riverside Park was created in part as an acknowledgement that the undulating, rocky coastline here would resist the rigid development of Manhattan's grid system. A plan by Central Park architect Frederick Law Olmsted was approved in 1875. He and Calvert Vaux worked on the park over the next quarter century, sculpting a landscape that left as many natural features as possible, such as Mount Tom. This was a favourite spot of Edgar Allan Poe, who lived in a nearby farmhouse and would come here to meditate and work on his poetry. While many places associated with Poe claim a connection to 'The Raven', it is very likely that he worked on it here.

9 Walk north on Riverside Drive five blocks to the Soldiers and Sailors Monument.

Three decades after the Civil War, the city began considering a memorial to the fallen. The Soldiers and Sailors Monument (a version of the Lysicrates Monument) was dedicated on Memorial Day, 1902. The pillars list New York's volunteer regiments, the major battles of the war and the most famous Union generals. The cannons overlooking the Hudson River are purely decorative—this spot was never used for defence. For the nearest subway, head to 86th Street and Broadway for the 1 train.

Artists' Upper West Side

Leafy side streets and avenues alive with activity reveal this neighbourhood's deep artistic roots, including the country's largest performing arts centre.

To many New Yorkers, the Upper West Side is seen as its 'arty' neighbourhood, which is in a way surprising, considering that this is a city that boasts SoHo, Chelsea and Greenwich Village among its list of important arts enclaves. Even the Upper East Side, with its many museums, *should* have a greater claim, but the character of the Upper West Side is different. In part, this is due to Lincoln Center, the gigantic complex of theatres, which dominates the area. But it is also that Upper West Siders often hold non-traditional jobs (more so than people in any other place in America), which means that the neighbourhood is always abuzz with activity, whether it's a Wednesday morning or a Saturday afternoon. This is a great stroll to do in the late morning to finish just in time for lunch. In addition to the three places we've recommended, you'll be near countless other good restaurants. On weekends in sunny weather you may notice long queues in front of many of them; these people are waiting to have brunch, a time-honoured tradition on the Upper West Side.

Exit the A/C, B/D or 1 subway at the Columbus Circle Station to emerge in the heart of a busy intersection where you will see a host of public art.

In the centre of Columbus Circle is the 1892 statue of Christopher Columbus by Gaetano Russo paid for by the Italian-American community and unveiled as part of the 400th anniversary celebrations of the explorer's voyage to America. At the juncture of Central Park West and Broadway sits a replica of the Unisphere from the 1964 World's Fair (the original is in Queens). Allegedly when Donald Trump purchased the Gulf + Western building (now the Trump International Hotel), a *feng shui* master suggested a globe to correct the tower's alignment. At the entrance to Central Park is the monument to the *USS Maine,* the naval vessel that went down in Cuba in 1898, sparking the Spanish–American War. The gilded figure on top of the pillar is the goddess Columbia emerging from the sea. It is actually cast from munitions salvaged from the *Maine* after the war. On the south side, Edward Durell Stone's former Huntington Hartford Museum is currently undergoing renovation to become the new home for the Museum of Arts and Design. Jazz at Lincoln Center, designed by Rafael Viñoly, is located within the gleaming Time Warner towers (which also contain a number of amenities including shops, a hotel, apartments and restaurants).

2 Leave Columbus Circle and walk 3 blocks north on Broadway to Dante

WHERE TO EAT

🍴 BOUCHON BAKERY,
in the Time Warner Center
at 59th Street;
Tel: 212-823-9366.
Thomas Keller's fancy take-away café.

🍴 HARRY'S BURRITOS,
241 Columbus Avenue
(at 71st Street);
Tel: 212-580-9494.
Hearty portions of Mexican (and Tex-Mex) favourites.

🍴 CAFÉ MOZART,
154 West 70th Street (at Broadway);
Tel: 212-595-9797.
Everything from simple pastries to full dinner in a music-filled space.

Park, from which there is an excellent view of the main plaza of Lincoln Center.

Tiny Dante Park was created to house Ettore Ximenes' 1921 statue of the poet, created to honour the 600th anniversary of his death. It now serves as the gateway to the Lincoln Center for the Performing Arts, America's premier theatrical complex. The building to the left (by Philip Johnson, 1964) is the New York State Theater and is home to the New York City Ballet and City Opera. The building to right is Avery Fisher Hall (Max Abramovitz, 1962), home to the New York Philharmonic. In the Center is the majestic Metropolitan Opera House

OPPOSITE: UNISPHERE IN COLUMBUS CIRCLE

149

DISTANCE 1.5 miles (2.45km)

ALLOW 1 hour

START **Columbus Circle station, A/C, B/D and 1 trains**

FINISH **72nd Street station, 1/2/3 trains**

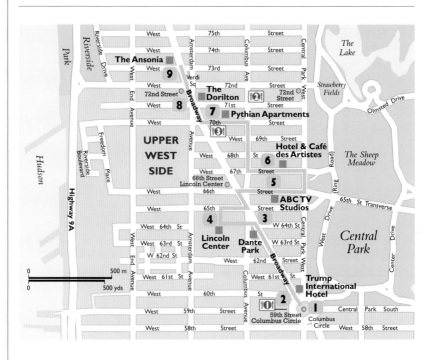

(Wallace K. Harrison, 1966), which also hosts the American Ballet Theater. (For those keeping track, that's *two* opera companies and *two* ballet companies side by side.) The Opera House features fantastic Marc Chagall murals (*The Sources of Music* and *The Triumph of Music*) kept hidden from sun damage during the day by large curtains. It is worth noting that before the complex was built, this working-class area, known as San Juan Hill, served as the setting for the 1961 musical *West Side Story*; indeed, it was filmed in abandoned tenements just before they were razed to the ground for Lincoln Center's construction. Near the fountain once stood the building that housed Aaron Copland's studio, where he wrote *Rodeo* and other classics.

LINCOLN CENTER; TEL: 212-875-5000

3 Cross Columbus Avenue at 64th Street to head into Lincoln Center's main plaza. Keep right (behind Avery Fisher Hall) to come to the pool in front of the Vivian Beaumont Theater.

Lincoln Center also houses both a Broadway and an Off-Broadway theatre, the performing arts branch of the New York Public Library, smaller performance venues (such as Alice Tully Hall) and one of the country's best music and art schools, Juilliard. The sculpture in the centre of the pool is Henry Moore's *Reclining Figure* from 1965, which contrasts nicely to the stark lines of the buildings that surround it.

4 Leave Lincoln Center via 65th Street and walk to Broadway. Walk one block north to 66th Street, then cross both Broadway and Columbus Avenues and continue east to the ABC Television Studios at 56 West 66th Street (on your right).

This ornate castle was built to be the First Battery Armory in 1901. Since 1976, when it was decommissioned, it has been a studio for ABC, who moved in just as the network was reaching a creative and popular zenith with the television mini-series *Roots*. Many popular ABC news and entertainment shows are still filmed here and in the block-long studio space across the street.

5 Continue on 66th Street to Central Park West. Turn left, walk one block, and turn left again onto 67th Street for the Hotel and Café des Artistes.

The Hotel des Artistes opened in 1918 and quickly became popular as an artists residence. Among those who called this home were Berenice Abbott, Norman Rockwell, Charlie Chaplin, Noel Coward and Howard Chandler Christy. If you peek in the windows of Café des Artistes on the ground floor, you can see Christy's murals of scantily clad women that he donated to the restaurant in lieu of paying his bill. Other artists' residences line the block. Perhaps the most important is the Atelier at 33 West 67th where Marcel Duchamp created his groundbreaking work, *The Bride Stripped Bare by Her Bachelors, Even*, for his patrons, Walter and Louise Arensberg, who were footing his $58 monthly rent.

6 Walk west to Columbus Avenue and turn right. Walk three blocks and turn left onto 70th Street and walk to the Pythian Apartments at 135 West 70th Street, which is best seen from across the street.

The Knights of Pythias were founded in 1864 as a fraternal and semi-secret society to promote friendship, charity and benevolence. Due to the organization's vaguely oriental flavour, membership swelled in the 1920s in the wake of Howard Carter's discovery of Tutankhamen's tomb and this building opened in 1927. Note the hotchpotch of ancient figures, including Assyrian lions and, at the top floor, large seated Pharaohs. After the Pythians moved out, part of the building became a recording studio and Bill Haley cut 'Rock Around the Clock' here. It is now luxury condos.

7 Continue to Broadway, turn right and walk one block north to the corner of 71st Street. The building on the north side is the Dorilton.

In 1902, the *Architectural Record* condemned this apartment building as so terrible it would make 'strong men swear and weak women shrink affrighted'. The vaguely Second Empire French design features a bracketed cornice on the fourth floor, large male figures holding up the bay windows and a massive mansard roof. It was opened here to take advantage of the brand-new subway, which opened in 1904 one block away.

8 Continue up Broadway to Verdi Square, the small park bounded by Amsterdam Avenue, Broadway, 72nd and 73rd Streets.

This marble statue of Verdi by Pasquale Civiletti, unveiled on Columbus Day in 1906, was built with funds raised by the Italian-American newspaper, *Il Progresso*. The figures that ring the base are characters from *Aida, Falstaff, Otello* and *La Forza del Destino*.

9 Visible from Verdi Square is The Ansonia across 73rd Street.

The Ansonia, opened in 1904, offered top-drawer amenities, including telephone service and artificial refrigeration in each apartment, maid service three times daily, and—in the ornate lobby fountain—live seals. Early advertisements for the building call it 'the largest and most completely appointed apartment hotel in the world'. The building's thick walls appealed to musicians: Arturo Toscanini, Enrico Caruso and Lily Pons all lived here. So did New York Yankees great Babe Ruth, who was evidently the world's worst saxophone player.

The entrance to the 1/2/3 subway is here in Verdi Square.

Morningside Heights

Once an isolated rural plateau, Morningside Heights grew in a unique way and is dominated by its churches, parks and academic institutions.

In the years following the Civil War, as Manhattan's northward growth enveloped the small Upper West Side village of Bloomingdale and the farmland in Harlem, the hill above 110th Street remained undeveloped and unnamed. The area was considered inaccessible—tall cliffs defined its western flank along the Hudson (the 'riverside') and even taller ones cascaded down the eastern edge (or 'morningside'). The only large landholder of note was the Bloomingdale Insane Asylum, whose rural 60-acre campus sprawled across most of the high plateau. The late 1880s brought rapid change. Three institutions—each associated with the Episcopal (Anglican) Church—decided to build large new homes in the rarefied air of the heights. By the dawn of the 20th century, a new cathedral was underway, a new hospital had been built, and the campus of the city's oldest university had completely recreated the new Morningside Heights and almost no trace of the pastoral plateau remained. Today, this residential neighbourhood is still defined by its institutional landowners as well as its rugged topography.

Exit the 1 subway at 110th Street and walk two blocks north on Broadway to 112th Street. Turn right and walk one block east to Amsterdam Avenue and the Cathedral Church of St John the Divine.

The rural character of Morningside Heights changed quickly in the 1890s when the Episcopal Church proposed this grand cathedral overlooking the city. Architects Heins & LaFarge drew up plans for an elaborate Romanesque/Byzantine design. Work began in 1892, but by 1907 not even the chancel and choir were complete. When Heins died that year, it cancelled the contract, leaving the cathedral free to hire Ralph Adams Cram, who promised to finish the job faster, and in a grander, Gothic style. Cram's soaring nave was completed in 1941, days before America entered World War II. Decorative stonework and partial construction of the south tower are all that have happened since. The cathedral, the world's largest, is worth exploring in detail. At the chancel end, take note of Heins & LaFarge's gigantic granite columns. In the nave, many stained-glass windows explore particularly American or modern themes. A window on the north wall is dedicated to John Jacob Astor IV—who perished on the *Titanic*—and shows the ship sinking in its lower right corner. Of particular note is a window on the south side that shows a 1920s singer at a radio microphone and, just above that, a man scrutinizing a small box—the first artistic depiction of the television. Back outside, the massive front

entry doors are surrounded by figures designed by a stone-carving workshop run by the cathedral in the 1980s. Below each saint are vignettes including a New York skyline showing the World Trade Center and an odd scene of traffic plummeting off a collapsing Brooklyn Bridge. A walk through the gardens south of the cathedral brings you to an 1843 Greek Revival building that is the oldest in the neighbourhood.

CATHEDRAL CHURCH OF ST JOHN THE DIVINE; TEL: 212-316-7490

2 Continue north on Amsterdam Avenue to 113th Street and turn right. Walk halfway down the block and stop opposite the original entrance to St Luke's Hospital.

WHERE TO EAT

🍽 TOM'S RESTAURANT,
2880 Broadway (at 112th Street);
Tel: 212-864-6137.
Diner made famous by Suzanne Vega and Seinfeld.

🍽 HUNGARIAN PASTRY SHOP,
1030 Amsterdam Avenue (between 110th and 111th Streets);
Tel: 212-866-4230.
The neighbourhood hangout.

🍽 MILL,
2895 Broadway (at 113th Street);
Tel: 212-666-7653.
Korean restaurant that was once a diner and still serves Lime Rickeys.

DISTANCE 1.65 miles (2.65km)

ALLOW 1.5 hours

START 110th Street station, 1 train

FINISH 116th Street station, 1 train

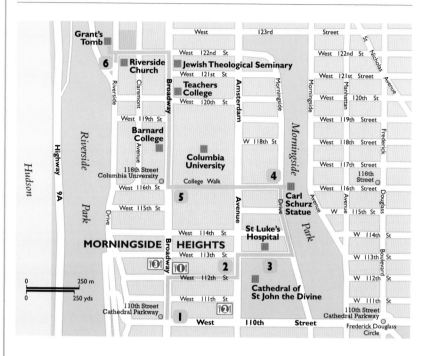

At the same time as the Episcopal diocese was planning its cathedral, the church–affiliated hospital was eyeing a move to a more modern facility, across the street from the cathedral. This 1896 building by Ernest Flagg includes an innovative series of wings connected through a central tower that prefigured the design of most modern American hospitals. Today, the western end of the building is obscured by a modern emergency wing, but the rest of the building retains its handsome Beaux Arts styling.

3 Continue on 113th Street to Morningside Drive. Turn left and walk three blocks north to the statue of Carl Schurz that sits just inside Morningside Park at 116th Street.

Morningside Park was built sporadically between 1870 and 1895 by Jacob Wrey Mould, Calvert Vaux and Frederick Law Olmsted. The expansive view here reveals just how much higher Morningside Heights is from the surrounding area in Harlem. The statue here is of German

newspaper editor Carl Schurz, who served as a Union General in the Civil War and went on to become the first German-American member of the US Senate. In 1968, Columbia University broke ground on a new gymnasium in the park. In April, Columbia students, upset that the city was giving up public land for private use and that the mostly black population in Harlem would have only nominal public access, launched an unprecedented eight-day campus take-over. The gym was abandoned; the original foundations at the bottom of the cliff now form a lovely waterfall.

4 Exit the park on 116th Street and walk one block west to Amsterdam Avenue. Cross Amsterdam Avenue onto College Walk and continue west halfway across campus. As you do so, the narrow corridor will suddenly widen, revealing **Low Memorial Library to the right and Butler Library to the left.**

Founded by royal charter in 1754 as King's College, the university changed its name after the American Revolution to the more patriotic-sounding Columbia. By the early 1890s, Columbia President Seth Low was campaigning to move the school to the area owned by the Bloomingdale Insane Asylum and to create a grand, expansive campus. Charles McKim's master plan for the campus is best seen in the area north of College Walk. Here, symmetrically paired academic buildings of stone and brick flank a grand limestone temple (modelled on Rome's Pantheon) that originally housed the school's library. When Low became too small, Butler Library (directly opposite on the south side of College Walk) was constructed and Low became the university's administrative headquarters. As you face Low Library, notice an out-of-character brick building to the right. This is Macy Villa (now Buell Hall), the only asylum building not to have been torn down.

COLUMBIA UNIVERSITY;
TEL: 212-854-1754

5 Continue through Columbia's campus on College Walk to the gate on Broadway. Turn right on Broadway and walk north to the corner of 122nd Street. As you walk, you will see a number of other institutions that give Morningside Heights its academic character. On the west side of Broadway are Columbia's sister school, Barnard College (116-120 Streets), Union Theological Seminary (120-121 Streets) and the Manhattan School of Music (121-122 Streets). On the east side are Teachers College (120-121 Streets) and the Jewish Theological Seminary (121-122 Streets). At 122nd Street, turn left and walk two blocks to Riverside Drive. Turn left to the main entrance of Riverside Church.

In the late 1920s, the Park Avenue Baptist Church, at the urging of its pastor Harry Emerson Fosdick and its wealthiest congregant, John D. Rockefeller, Jr, announced plans to create an interdenominational, liberally progressive church on Morningside Heights. This was only after Rockefeller had donated $500,000 to the Cathedral of St John the Divine hoping for a seat on its vestry. The cathedral took the

money, but rebuffed Rockefeller, causing him to quickly finance Riverside Church. Whereas the cathedral, constructed using medieval stone-on-stone techniques, is today still years away from completion, Riverside Church, built as a steel-frame skyscraper, was finished in under six years. The carillon at the top of the bell tower contains the world's largest cast bell, which weighs 20 tons (18,144kg).

6 Cross Riverside Drive to the plaza in front of Grant's Tomb.

Ulysses S. Grant was one of the most revered men of his generation. The respect he earned for winning the Civil War carried him through two fairly unimpressive terms as America's president and into a retirement in New York. He lost all his money in bad investments and worked feverishly to complete his memoirs before dying of throat cancer in 1885. Other cities lobbied for the right to bury the former president, but New York had been his last home and planned to commemorate its new favourite son by building the largest mausoleum in America. The tomb, completed in 1897, is by John Duncan and is modelled on the mausoleum at Halicanarssus, one of the seven wonders of the ancient world. Inside, Grant and his wife Julia are entombed on the lower level in Napoleonic porphyry sarcophagi.

GENERAL GRANT NATIONAL MEMORIAL; DAILY 9-5; TEL: 212-666-1640
www.nps.gov/gegr

Retrace your steps to Broadway at 116th Street and the 1 train.

WALK 23

Harlem and Hamilton Heights

This area of Central Harlem rose to prominence between 1880 and 1920 and has some of the grandest homes and churches in New York.

Synonymous with jazz and the Harlem Renaissance, this area has a history that stretches back to the 17th-century Dutch village of 'New Haarlem'. One of Manhattan's largest neighbourhoods, Harlem cuts a diagonal path across the island from 155th Street on the west to 96th Street on the east. Our walk focuses on central Harlem and begins in Hamilton Heights. Harlem's rural character changed with the coming of the horse-drawn railroad in 1837. Additional transportation improvements—the elevated railway in 1879; the subway in 1904—led to increased development. The neighbourhood was designed for upper middle class white New Yorkers. When they didn't come in sufficient numbers, German and Eastern European immigrants moved in, but only after World War I did a significant black population begin to arrive, pushed out of the 'Tenderloin' on Manhattan's west side below 42nd Street. Known since the 1920s as America's premier black neighbourhood, the area has always drawn an eclectic mix, both economically and ethnically.

Exit the A/C and B/D subway at 145th Street. Head west (uphill) one block to Convent Avenue and turn left. Walk south to the block between 144th and 143rd Streets.

These massive homes, dating from the 1880s and 90s, have impressive high stoops, which originally masked servants' entrances beneath. The homes on the east side were built by Adolph Hoak. Rather than a bland, 'one-size-fits-all' approach, Hoak mixed eclectic riffs on Dutch revival and mock Tudor and then added a variety of stonework to differentiate his designs. This is part of the Hamilton Heights historic district, and these are some of the best late 19th-century townhouses preserved in the city.

2 Continue one block south on Convent Avenue to the Hamilton Grange National Memorial.

This quaint 1802 farmhouse was built by America's first Treasury Secretary, Alexander Hamilton, to provide a country retreat from downtown's yellow fever outbreaks. Hamilton worked near Wall Street and commuted, even though it was at least two hours by stagecoach. The Grange, named after Hamilton's family home in Scotland (on which he'd never set eyes), wasn't originally here—it was moved here in 1889 from its previous location on 143rd Street. Now administered by the National Parks Service, the house is currently closed as preparations are underway to move it yet again, to nearby St Nicholas Park.

3 Continue two blocks south on Convent Avenue to City College. Enter the north gates and pause in the centre of the campus.

City College is the oldest of the 23 schools in New York's City University system. Founded in 1847 as the Free Academy of the City of New York, it offered free education, primarily to the children of immigrants. It moved to Harlem in 1906, following the opening of the first line of the subway. Indeed, architect George B. Post used debris from the subway tunneling to build the Gothic quadrangle. Each building mimics one part of a medieval walled city, with Shepard Hall (on the east side of campus) playing the role of the cathedral. At the time of its move to Harlem, the college was becoming predominantly Jewish and, in the early years of the 20th century, increasingly radical, earning it the nickname the 'Harvard of the Proletariat'.

CITY COLLEGE; TEL: 212-650-7000

DISTANCE 2.3 miles (3.7 km)

ALLOW 1.5 hours

START 145th Street station, A/C and B/D trains

FINISH 125th Street station, A/C and B/D trains

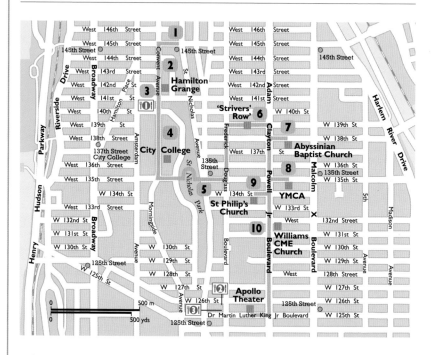

4 Continue south on Convent Avenue to 135th Street. Turn left, and walk one block to St Nicholas Park. Enter the park at the staircase and proceed down the stairs to the bottom of the hill.

This narrow park was built to help the city deal with the grade change from the top of Hamilton Heights to the expanse of lower Harlem. It was landscaped in 1906 in the rustic, picturesque style popularized by Calvert Vaux and Frederick Law Olmsted in Central Park.

5 Cross St Nicholas Avenue and walk one block east on 135th Street to Frederick Douglass Boulevard. Turn left (north) on Frederick Douglass to 139th Street. As you walk, note the service alley between 138th and 139th Streets, then turn right onto 139th Street and the King Model Houses, otherwise known as 'Strivers' Row'.

David King was one of New York's most successful contractors. In 1891, he decided to try his hand at real estate

development and commissioned Stanford White (who had built the Washington Memorial Arch), James Lord and Bruce Price to design a total of 146 houses over two blocks. White's homes line the north side of 139th Street, while the homes opposite are by Price. The development continues on 138th Street with homes by Price and Lord. King's timing could not have been worse—the financial panic of 1893 led to foreclosure when he'd sold just nine homes. By World War I, most were rented to blacks who were forced out of Midtown by the building of the new Pennsylvania Railroad station, and the area became known as Strivers' Row. While some whites used the term disparagingly, those who lived here took it as a sign of great pride. Notice that Stanford White's houses lack the usual entry stoop. White reasoned that as these homes all had actual back doors, high stoops that concealed servants' entrances were unnecessary. By contrast, Bruce Price's homes on the south side still feature the broad staircase, which had long been considered a status symbol.

6 Walk east on 139th Street until you reach Adam Clayton Powell Jr Boulevard and turn right. Walk one block south, and turn left onto 138th Street to view the Abyssinian Baptist Church at 132 West 138th, currently the most famous church in Harlem.

The second oldest black congregation in New York, Abyssinian Baptist was founded in 1808 in protest over racial segregation; in white churches blacks—free and enslaved—were forced to sit in a 'slave's gallery' upstairs. In the 1930s, Abyssinian Baptist became the largest protestant church in the world. The parish's most famous pastor was politician Adam Clayton Powell, Jr, who was elected to the US House of Representatives in 1944—the first black to represent Harlem—and served until just before his death in 1972. Powell was a great force of positive change in the neighbourhood. He rose to prominence by leading a boycott of Harlem stores where blacks could shop but were barred from employment. The slogan 'Don't Shop Where You Can't Work' was instrumental in breaking down the colour line in New York and in cities around the country. The nearby boulevard was named in memory of him.

7 Return to Adam Clayton Powell Jr Boulevard, walk south three blocks, and turn left onto 135th Street to stand in front of the Harlem YMCA at 180 West 135th Street.

Because black visitors to New York were refused service in most white-run hotels, the YMCA served as a gathering place for artists and entertainers. James Baldwin, Ralph Ellison and Langston Hughes all rented rooms here. In fact, Hughes introduced Ellison to author Richard Wright, who encouraged him to abandon music in favour of literature.

8 Return to Adam Clayton Powell Jr Boulevard, turn left and walk one block south to 134th Street. Cross to the far side of the boulevard and walk west a few doors to St Philip's Church at 204 West 134th Street.

St Philip's was built in 1910 by Tandy & Foster, the first African-American architecture firm to be licensed in New York. In an era when white landowners were reluctant to sell to blacks, the pastor of the church, Hutchens Bishop, was able to acquire this land and a row of nearby apartments for his parishioners because he was light-skinned and able to 'pass'. The wholesale relocation of St Philip's from the Tenderloin neighbourhood to Harlem was the first step in the shift of the neighbourhood from white to mainly black. By 1950, this was the single largest Episcopal congregation in America.

9 Return to Adam Clayton Powell Jr Boulevard. Turn south and walk two blocks to the Williams CME Church and the Tree of Hope.

In 1913, the new Lafayette Theatre (now the Williams CME Church) broke the colour line, inviting black audiences to enjoy its repertory of classic plays in the same seats and for the same prices as whites. Its fame skyrocketed in the 1930s with the Negro Theater Project production of 20-year-old Orson Welles' all-black *Macbeth*. In the median is a colourful statue commemorating the 'tree of hope', an old chestnut tree that performers would rub for good luck. After the original tree was cut down, a portion was preserved just off stage at the Apollo Theater. It remains a talisman.

WHERE TO EAT

|O| CAFÉ ONE,
1619 Amsterdam Avenue
(at 140th Street);
Tel: 212-234-3964.
Coffee, sandwiches and breakfast pastries.

|O| ROTI PLUS,
2345 Frederick Douglass Boulevard (between 125th and 126th Streets);
Tel: 212-749-8758.
Traditional Caribbean fare in an airy, inviting space.

|O| MANNAS,
2331 Frederick Douglass Boulevard (at 125th Street);
Tel: 212-749-9084.
Soul food buffet with a seating area upstairs.

10 Continue walking south on Adam Clayton Powell Boulevard to 125th Street. Turn right and walk half a block to the Apollo Theater.

The Apollo Theater opened in 1914 (as a burlesque house); its famous amateur night launched in 1934 and Ella Fitzgerald was an early winner. Other famous singers whose careers were boosted by their Apollo appearances include Billie Holiday, James Brown, Michael Jackson and Stevie Wonder.

For the nearest subway, walk one block east to the A/C and B/D 125th Street station at St Nicholas Avenue.

America's First Suburb

Brooklyn Heights, the city's first protected historic district, is known for its quiet streets, graceful churches—and superb view of Manhattan.

Until the beginning of the 19th century, most of Brooklyn was farmland. Commercial piers developed along the East River and eventually, in 1834, this area became the city of Brooklyn. By the end of the 19th century, Brooklyn was the third largest city in America. However, on 1 January 1898, Brooklyn lost its status as an independent city (a move some Brooklynites resent to this day) and was absorbed into New York. Brooklyn has always defined itself as different from Manhattan: more rural, pious, and quiet than its neighbour across the river. Nowhere is that more apparent than Brooklyn Heights, which developed rapidly in the first two decades of the 19th century as a commuter suburb for people working in Lower Manhattan. Part of the charm of this neighbourhood is simply experiencing the streetscape. Take time to notice the differences in house design. Every period, from Federal to Queen Anne to Romanesque Revival, is represented on these streets. To see the beautiful church interiors, take this tour on a Sunday in the late morning as services are finishing.

1 Exit the Borough Hall 2/3 and 4/5 subway station. Proceed to the far side of Cadman Plaza towards the statue of Henry Ward Beecher.

The most famous Brooklynite of the 19th century was preacher Henry Ward Beecher, an ardent abolitionist. While the name of his sister, Harriet Beecher Stowe (the author of *Uncle Tom's Cabin*) may be more famous today, Beecher was one of the most important men in America. This statue, by J.Q.A. Ward, is among the sculptor's finest. Literally putting Beecher on a pedestal, Ward surrounds him with a freed slave and a pair of children (and, by extension, the viewer). The children garland the statue with flowers—a tradition for statues of fallen soldiers—thus elevating the civilian preacher to the level of a Civil War combatant.

2 Turn around and walk towards the magnificent Borough Hall.

When Brooklyn incorporated in 1834, the new city held a contest to design City Hall, but winner Calvin Pollard was only able to lay foundations before the city ran out of funds. Ten years later, builder/grocer Gamaliel King, who had been the runner up, was hired to build his own version—as long as it could fit on Pollard's foundations. The result is one of the most elegant Greek Revival structures in New York. The dome is an 1898 addition—the same year this building was demoted from City Hall to Borough Hall when Brooklyn was annexed into the new Greater City of New York.

3 Leave Cadman Plaza via Montague Street. Walk one block west on Montague Street to 177 Montague, the Chase Bank.

The greatest bank architects in New York were York & Sawyer, and this 1915 structure—originally the Brooklyn Trust Company—is a splendid example of their work. The exterior is modelled on a Renaissance palazzo; the interior is classical, with a soaring coffered ceiling and a frieze of Roman gods circling the interior. If visiting during regular business hours, go inside to admire the terrazzo floor, the chandeliers, and the original furnishings. *No photos, please!*

4 Look across Clinton Street at the Church of St Ann and the Holy Trinity.

Opened in 1848, architect Minard Lafever's Church of the Holy Trinity (the 'St Ann' was added later) was paid for in its entirety by one wealthy parishioner, Edgar Bartow. Bartow insisted on American stained-glass windows. They were designed by William Bolton and are the first such examples in America. Lafever is often overlooked in a city that boasted James Renwick and Richard Upjohn among its roster of ecclesiastical builders, but this is one of the best Gothic Revival churches in the city.

5 Turn right onto Clinton Street and walk one block to Pierrepoint Street and the Brooklyn (formerly Long Island) Historical Society.

DISTANCE **1.5 miles (2.45km)**

ALLOW **1.5 hours**

START **Borough Hall station, 2/3 and 4/5 trains**

FINISH **Clark Street station, 2/3 trains**

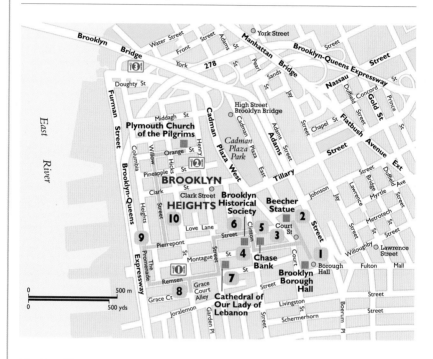

The Brooklyn Historical Society offers a great example of how the borough differed from Manhattan, for the institution's charter came from the New England Historical Society in Boston, not from the New-York Historical Society just across the river. This headquarters, designed by George B. Post, opened in 1881. The portrait busts that dot the façade personify the aims of the Society. Along Clinton Street are Michelangelo, Beethoven, Gutenberg and Shakespeare. On the Pierrepont Street side are two figures important to American history: founding father Benjamin Franklin and Christopher Columbus. Flanking the door are a sailor and a Native American, typical allegories of the city's past.

BROOKLYN HISTORICAL SOCIETY;
WED–SUN 12-5; TEL: 718-222-4111;
www.brooklynhistory.org

6 Walk one block on Pierrepont Street to Henry Street. Turn left and proceed two blocks south to the Cathedral of Our Lady of Lebanon.

WHERE TO EAT

🍽 **TERESA'S,**
80 Montague Street (at Hicks);
Tel: 718-797-3996.
Brooklyn outpost of the famous
East Village Polish eatery.

🍽 **SIGGY'S,**
76 Henry Street (between
Pineapple and Orange Streets);
Tel: 718-237-3199.
Organic food in a homey atmosphere
(closed Tue).

🍽 **GRIMALDI'S,**
19 Old Fulton Street (between
Front and Water Streets);
Tel: 718-858-4300.
Brooklyn's most-famous pizza place;
expect to wait for a table.

This was originally the Church of the
Pilgrims, an important Congregational
parish. To establish this congregation's
bona fides as descendents of America's
original Puritans, a piece of the Plymouth
Rock was chiselled off and set in the
building's cornerstone. However, in
1934, with church attendance in decline,
this parish merged with Henry Ward
Beecher's nearby Plymouth Church,
taking the Plymouth Rock corner stone,
Tiffany Windows and even the doors
with them. Thus, when the Lebanese
Catholic church purchased this property,
they needed to completely redecorate.
Look, in particular, at the entrance on
Remsen Street: the panels show castles

and a steamship being towed into port.
All these doors come from the formal
dining room on the *SS Normandie* and
had been removed during World War
II when the ship was refitted as a troop
transport vessel.

7 Walk one block west on Remsen
Street to Hicks Street. Turn left and
continue one short block to Grace
Court Alley.

This quaint mews was a selling point.
In a city where most homes lacked
carriage drives, the houses on Remsen
and Joralemon Streets connected to this
stabling mews commanded a premium
price. All have now been converted into
private homes, but retain a number of
original features, including hay cranes
above some of the former stable doors.

8 Retrace your steps to Remsen,
then turn left and walk one block
to The Promenade.

When the Brooklyn–Queens Expressway
was built in the 1940s, this esplanade
was added to reduce highway noise and
provide public access to this spectacular
view of Manhattan. Before the Brooklyn
Bridge—seen beautifully from here—was
built, staircases led down this steep cliff to
ferry docks where commuters travelled
to the financial district. On good days,
this was only a few minutes' journey; in
bad weather, however, the trip sometimes
didn't happen at all. The Brooklyn Bridge
forever changed Brooklyn's relationship
to Manhattan by providing constant

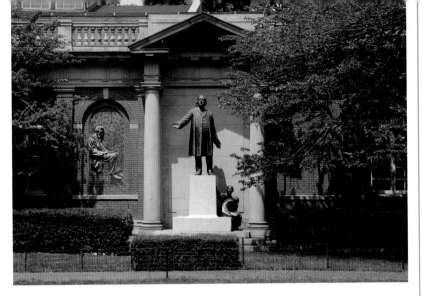

access. Then only 15 years after it opened, the two cities merged into one.

9 After strolling along The Promenade, leave via Pierrepont Street. Walk one block and turn left for 155-159 Willow Street.

These three homes and the adjoining stable are the best examples of Federal architecture in the neighbourhood. Particularly intriguing is the skylight in front of No. 157, which illuminates an underground passage between the house and stable so the owners could retrieve their carriage in bad weather. This may also have been a stop on the Underground Railroad, a series of safe houses used to smuggle fugitive slaves from southern states to Canada in the era leading up to the Civil War. (The nearby Plymouth Church was definitely a stop, known as the 'Grand Central' for runaway slaves.)

10 Walk three blocks to Orange Street, turn right and walk two blocks to reach the Plymouth Church of the Pilgrims.

Known as the Plymouth Church of the Pilgrims since its merger with the parish on Henry Street, this was the pulpit of Henry Ward Beecher for nearly 40 years. A statue of Beecher by Gutzon Borglum (of Mount Rushmore fame) stands in the churchyard. One of the slaves on the pedestal is Sally Maria Diggs, known as 'Pinky', sold by Beecher in a mock auction at the church that shed stark light on the treatment of humans as chattel. Borglum's bas relief of Abraham Lincoln is set in the wall to the left; Lincoln's appearance at this church in February 1860 helped him get elected later that year. For the nearest subway, continue on Orange Street to Henry Street and turn right. Walk two blocks to the Clark Street 2/3 station.

171

INDEX

ABC Television Studios 152
Abyssinian Baptist Church 164
The Alamo 51
B. Altman Building 96
American Museum of Natural
    History 142–3
The Ansonia 153
Apollo Theater 165
The Apthorp 144
Asia Society 121
Astor, John Jacob 50, 55, 100
Astor Library 55

Banca Stabile 37
Bayard-Condict Building 54
Beecher, Henry Ward 167,
    170, 171
Belvedere Castle 135
Bethesda Terrace 135, 138
Boathouse, Central Park 138
Bohemian National Hall 116
Borough Hall, Brooklyn 167
Bow Bridge 138–9
Bowery 50, 52–4, 57
Bowling Green Park 9
Broadway 8, 92
Brooklyn 166–71
Brooklyn Bridge 18–19, 170–1
Brooklyn Heights 166-171
Brooklyn Historical Society
    167–8
Bryant Park 100
Butler Library 158

Carl Schurz Park 116–17
Carousel, Central Park 129
Castle Clinton 13
Cathedral of St John the
    Divine 155, 159
Central Park 125, 126–131,
    134–9, 140
Chelsea 84–9
Chelsea Market 85
Chelsea Piers 87
Chinatown 28–33
Christopher Park 68

Chrysler Building 96, 102
Chumley's 66–8
Church of the Ascension
    60–1
Church of the Incarnation 95
Church of the Most Precious
    Blood 37
Church of St Ann and the Holy
    Trinity 167
Church of St Luke in the Fields
    65
Church of San Salvatore 39
Church of the Transfiguration
    (Mott Street) 33
Church of the Transfiguration
    (35th Street) 95
City Beautiful movement
    58–60
City College 161
City Hall 18
Colonnade Row 55
Columbia University 158–9
Columbus Circle 149
Columbus Park 29
Conservatory Water 138
Cooper-Hewitt National
    Design Museum 124–5
Cooper Union 51

Da Gennaro Restaurant 37
Dairy, Central Park 127-9
The Dakota 140, 141
Dante Park 149
The Dorilton 153
Doyers Street 31
Dylan, Bob 37, 89

East Village 70–5
Educational Alliance 23
Eldridge Street Synagogue
    25–6
Electric Circus 73
Empire State Building 96, 102
Engine/Ladder Company
    Ten 15-16
Essex Street 26–7

Evelyn Apartments 143–4
Fabbri mansion 113
Fifth Avenue 56, 120, 140
Five Points 29–31
Flagg, Ernest 43, 55, 156
Flatiron Building 93
Foley Square 19
Forward Building 23
42nd Street 98–103
Fraunces Tavern 12–13
'Freedom Tower' 15
Frick Collection 120, 121

Gangs of New York 30
Gay Street 69
General Motors Building 110
General Slocum 70, 73, 74
General Theological Seminary
    88–9
German American Shooting
    Society 72
Gilbert, Cass 9, 18, 19, 122
Gotti, John 40
Grace Court Alley 170
Gracie Mansion 112, 117
Gramercy Park 78–83
Grand Central Terminal
    100–2
Grant's Tomb 159
Greenwich Village 56–61,
    64–9, 70
'Ground Zero' 14
Grove Court 65
Guggenheim Museum 124

Hamilton, Alexander 10, 125,
    161
Hamilton Grange 161
Hamilton Heights 160–2
Harlem 160–5
Harlem YMCA 164
Harmonie Club 113
Haughwout, E.V. 43
Hell's Angels clubhouse 74
Henderson Place 116
Herter Brothers 29, 39

Hotel des Artistes 152
Hotel Chelsea 89
IAC/InterActive 86
Irving, Washington 55, 79, 83, 114

Jan Hus Church 116
Jarmulowsky's Bank 25
Jefferson Market 61
Johnson, Philip 107, 110, 149

Kehila Kedosha Janina 26
King Model Houses 162–4
Kletzker Brotherly Aid Association 24
Knickerbocker Club 113–14

Lafayette Theatre 165
LaGuardia, Fiorello 100, 117, 130
Lake, Central Park 138
Lennon, John 130, 141
Lever House 106, 107–8
Lincoln Center 148, 149–52
Little Italy 34–41
London Terrace 88
Low Library 158–9
Lower East Side 22–7
Lower Manhattan 8–13

McSorley's Old Ale House 51–2
Madison Square Park 92, 93
Mahayana Buddhist Temple 33
Mall, Central Park 129
Mercantile Exchange 46
Merchant's House Museum 52–4
Metropolitan Club 113
Metropolitan Life 93–4
Metropolitan Museum of Art 120, 122, 142
Metropolitan Opera House 149–50
Model Boat Pond 138
Morgan Library & Museum 95
Morningside Heights 154–9

Morningside Park 156–8
Mott Street 33
Mould, Jacob Wrey 122,130, 138, 142, 156
Mount Tom 144
Mulberry Bend 29
Mulberry Street 36, 40
Museum Mile 120–5
Museum of the Chinese in the Americas 29
Museum of the City of New York 125

National Arts Club 80-2
National Museum of the American Indian 9
Neue Gallerie 122–4
New Amsterdam 8, 12
New Victory Theater 99
New York City Marble Cemetery 74
New-York Historical Society 142, 168
New York Police Department Headquarters 38
New York Public Library 55, 73, 82, 100, 121, 152
New York Times headquarters 99–100
NoHo 50–5
NoLita 36, 40
Northern Dispensary 68

Obelisk, Central Park 136
Olmsted, Frederick Law 126–30, 134–5, 138–9, 144, 156, 162
Otis, Elisha 43, 100

Park Avenue 114
Patchin Place 69
Pete's Tavern 82
Plymouth Church 170, 171
Poe, Edgar Allan 68, 144
Post, George B. 12, 161, 168
Prince Street 43–5
The Promenade, Brooklyn 170–1

Public Theater 55
The Puck Building 40
Pythian Apartments 153

Radio City Music Hall 110
Ramble, Central Park 139
Ravenite Social Club 40
RCA Building 107
Riverside Church 159
Riverside Park 140, 144
Rockefeller Center 109
Roosevelt (Theodore) House 79
The Row 57–8

St James' Church 31
St Luke's Hospital 155–6
St Marks in the Bowery 71
St Mark's Place 72–3
St Nicholas Park 162
St Patrick's Cathedral 108–9
St Patrick's (Old) Cathedral 40
St Paul's Chapel 16
St Philip's Church 165
The San Remo 141
Seagram Building 106, 107
Shakespeare Garden 135
Sheep Meadow 129–30
Sheridan Square 68
'Shteibl Row' 23–4
Silk Stocking District 112–17
Singer Manufacturing Company 43
Slavery in New York 19, 40, 163, 167, 171
SoHo 42–7, 57
Soldiers and Sailors Monument 144
Starrett-Lehigh 87–8
Stonewall Inn 68
Strawberry Fields 130
'Strivers' Row' 162–4
Stuyvesant Square 83
Sullivan, Louis 54
Supreme Court building 94

Tavern on the Green 130

Temple Emanu-El 114

Tompkins Square Park 73

Triangle Shirtwaist Factory 57

TriBeCa 42, 46

Trinity Church 10–12

Trump Tower 110

Twin Towers 14–16

Ukrainian Institute of America 122

United Nations 102

University Settlement 26

Upjohn, Richard 10, 61, 167

Upper East Side 112–17, 140, 148

Upper West Side 140–5, 148–53

US Custom House 9

Vaux, Calvert 29, 80, 122, 126–30, 134–5, 138–9, 142, 144, 156, 162

Verdi Square 153

Village East Theater 71

Wall Street 12

Warhol, Andy 73, 89

Washington, George 12, 13, 16, 19, 60

Washington Mews 60

Washington Square 57–8

West 10th Street 61

West Broadway 45

West Village 64–9

White, Stanford 60, 61, 113, 143, 164

White House Hotel 54

Whitney Museum of American Art 121–2

Williams CME Church 165

Wollman Rink 127

Woolworth Building 18

World Trade Center 14–16

Wright, Frank Lloyd 107, 122, 124

ACKNOWLEDGEMENTS

The Automobile Association would like to thank the following photographers, companies and picture libraries for their assistance in the preparation of this book.

3 AA/ Richard Elliott; 6-7 AA; 8 Corbis/ John Frazee; 11 James & Michelle Nevius; 13 AA / Douglas Corrance; 14 James & Michelle Nevius; 15 James & Michelle Nevius; 17 AA/ Ellen Rooney; 18 AA/ Clive Sawyer; 20-21 AA/ Paul Kenward; 22 AA/ Richard Elliot; 23 James & Michelle Nevius; 25 James & Michelle Nevius; 26 P Deliss/Godong/Corbis; 27 James & Michelle Nevius; 28 AA/ Clive Sawyer; 29 James & Michelle Nevius; 31 James & Michelle Nevius; 32 Catherine Karnow/Corbis; 34-35 Jeff Eden; 36 Jeff Eden; 39 Frances M Roberts/ Alamy; 41 AA/ Clive Sawyer; 42 James & Michelle Nevius; 45 James & Michelle Nevius; 47 AA/ Clive Sawyer; 48-49 Jeff Eden; 50 Robert Holmes/Corbis; 51 Jeff Eden; 53 Jeff Eden; 54 Jeff Eden; 56 AA/ Simon McBride; 57 James & Michelle Nevius; 59 AA/ Paul Kenward; 60 James & Michelle Nevius; 62-63 Michael S. Yamashita/ Corbis; 64 AA/ Clive Sawyer; 67 Jeff Eden; 69 James & Michelle Nevius; 70 AA/ Richard Elliot; 74 Jeff Eden; 75 Jeff Eden; 76-77 AA/ Simon McBride; 78 Philip Scalia/Alamy; 79 James & Michelle Nevius; 81 James & Michelle Nevius; 83 James & Michelle Nevius; 84 Catherine Karnow/Corbis; 85 James & Michelle Nevius; 87 Jeff Eden; 89 AA/ Clive Sawyer; 90-91 Black Star/Alamy; 92 Photolibrary/ Eric Kamp; 93 AA/ Douglas Corrance; 95 James & Michelle Nevius; 97 AA/ Simon McBride; 98 AA/ Clive Sawyer; 103 AA/ Clive Sawyer; 104-105 AA/ Simon McBride; 106 Photolibrary Group Ltd; 107 Angelo Hornak/Corbis; 109 AA/Clive Sawyer; 111 AA/Clive Sawyer; 112 James & Michelle Nevius; 113 James & Michelle Nevius; 117 AA/ Clive Sawyer; 118-119 AA/Richard Elliott; 120 AA/Clive Sawyer; 121 Arcaid/Alamy; 124 AA/Richard Elliott; 126 Andrew Fox/ Alamy; 130 Alan Gallery/ Alamy; 131 AA/ Simon McBride; 132-133 AA/ Paul Kenward; 134 Henry Westheim Photography/ Alamy; 137 James & Michelle Nevius; 139 Sandra Baker/ Alamy; 140 Walter Bibikow/ Photolibrary; 143 AA/ Clive Sawyer; 145 James & Michelle Nevius; 146-147 James & Michelle Nevius; 148 James & Michelle Nevius; 151 Ambient Images Inc./Alamy; 152 James & Michelle Nevius; 154 Richard Levine/ Alamy; 157 Robert Harding Picture Library Ltd/ Alamy; 158 JTB Communications Inc./ Photolibrary; 160 Farrell Grehan/ Corbis; 161 James & Michelle Nevius; 163 James & Michelle Nevius; 166 Jeff Eden; 169 AA/ Douglas Corrance; 171 Jeff Eden; 172-173 Alan Gallery/ Alamy.

Every effort has been made to trace the copyright holders, and we apologise in advance for any accidental errors. We would be happy to apply the corrections in the following edition of this publication.